27 PATHS BACK TO LIFE

27 Paths Back to Life

Niko Riki

Contents

1

Daniel's Journey

The rhythmic hum of the car engine always brought Daniel a sense of calm. There was something meditative about being on the open road, with endless possibilities stretching ahead. On weekends, he often drove through the countryside, winding through golden fields and past quiet villages. The car wasn't just a vehicle to Daniel; it was freedom, escape, and adventure all rolled into one.

But one rainy evening, as he was driving home after a long day at work, everything changed. The sky was dark, and the roads were slick with rain. He had taken this route dozens of times before, but tonight, a sudden swerve to avoid an animal on the road led to chaos.

The tires screeched. The car skidded. Daniel's heart pounded as he struggled to regain control, but it was too late. The impact was deafening, and then—nothing.

When Daniel awoke, pain consumed him. His body felt like it was on fire, with every movement bringing sharp, unbearable agony. The sterile smell of the hospital and the beeping of machines surrounded him. Nurses and doctors moved in and out of the room, their faces kind but filled with concern.

The doctors explained the extent of his injuries—broken ribs, a fractured leg, and a concussion. The recovery process would be long and arduous. As the weeks dragged on, Daniel found himself sinking into a deep depression. The physical pain was overwhelming, but the emotional toll was worse.

"I'm broken," he thought, staring at the ceiling during another sleepless night.

Driving, which had once been his passion, now filled him with dread. He replayed the crash over and over in his mind, haunted by the screech of tires and the crushing impact.

One night, as Daniel lay in his hospital bed, the pain became too much to bear. He felt himself slipping into unconsciousness, his body and mind exhausted. What happened next would change his life forever.

Daniel found himself in a vast, dark tunnel. The walls seemed to shimmer with an ethereal light, and he felt a pull, as if something—or someone—was guiding him forward. At the end of the tunnel, a brilliant light awaited, warm and inviting. As he moved closer, Daniel saw figures standing in the light—angels, their forms radiant and otherworldly. Their presence filled him with a peace he had never known. A voice, deep and resonant, echoed through the space. It wasn't harsh or judgmental; it was kind and filled with love.

"Daniel," the voice said, "your journey is not over. There is more for you to do. Trust in the path that has been laid before you."

Tears streamed down Daniel's face as he felt the weight of those words. He wanted to stay in the light, to remain in this place of perfect peace, but the voice urged him back.

When he awoke, the hospital room felt different. The pain was still there, but so was a sense of purpose.

Recovering wasn't easy. Each day was a battle, both physically and emotionally. But Daniel held onto the memory of the tunnel, the light, and the voice that had spoken to him. Slowly, he began to see his struggles as part of a larger plan.

One of the biggest challenges was overcoming his fear of driving. Just the thought of getting behind the wheel made his hands shake and his heart race. Eventually, he made the decision to sell his car.

"It's not worth the anxiety," he told himself.

Instead, Daniel began taking the train. At first, it was just a practical solution, but over time, he grew to enjoy the slow, steady rhythm of the ride. The trains were a place of reflection, a chance to watch the world go by and let his thoughts wander.

It was on one of these train rides that Daniel noticed her for the first time. She sat by the window, her auburn hair catching the sunlight, her nose buried in a book. There was something serene about her presence, something that drew Daniel in.

After that day, he found himself looking forward to the train rides in a way he hadn't before. He and the woman—her name was Claire, as he later learned—began to exchange polite greetings. Small talk about the weather turned into longer conversations about books, music, and the landscapes they passed.

Claire had a laugh that was soft but infectious, and her curiosity about life made Daniel feel like the world was brighter when she was around. For the first time since the accident, he felt seen—not as a broken man but as someone who could heal.

On one train ride, Daniel opened up about his fear of driving. He described the crash and the overwhelming guilt and fear that had consumed him afterward. Claire listened intently, her eyes filled with empathy.

"You've been through so much," she said gently. "But look at you now—you're here, moving forward."

Her words stayed with him.

The train rides became their time. They would sit by the window together, watching the world blur by, and share stories from their lives. Claire told Daniel about her love of painting and how she found inspiration in the smallest details—like the way the light danced on the surface of a lake or the intricate veins of a leaf. Daniel found himself opening up about his dreams before the crash, dreams he had buried under layers of self-doubt.

One chilly autumn evening, as they walked from the station to a nearby coffee shop, Daniel realized how much Claire had become a part of his life. Her presence was like a light guiding him out of the shadows of his past.

As they sipped their drinks, Daniel took a deep breath. "Claire," he said, "meeting you has been the best thing that's happened to me in a long time."

She smiled, her cheeks tinged with a rosy hue. "I feel the same way."

Months passed, and their bond deepened. They explored new places together, visited art galleries, and spent quiet evenings by the fireplace, lost in conversation. Eventually, Daniel realized he didn't just want Claire to be a part of his life—he wanted her to be his life.

One crisp spring morning, on the very train where they had met, Daniel proposed. He knelt by the window seat, holding a small ring box, and asked Claire to marry him. Her joyful "Yes!" echoed in his heart, filling the space that had once been empty with love and hope.

Years later, as Daniel sat on the porch of their countryside home, he found himself reflecting on the journey that had brought him to this moment. The car crash, the pain, the fear—it had all felt insurmountable at the time. But without those experiences, he wouldn't have found Claire or the happiness they shared.

He looked out at the rolling hills, the golden light of the setting sun casting long shadows, and thought about how life had a way of leading people to where they were meant to be.

"Everything happens for a purpose," he murmured, a smile tugging at his lips.

Claire stepped out onto the porch, placing a hand on his shoulder. "What's that?"

"Nothing," he said, taking her hand in his. "Just thinking about how lucky I am."

2

———————————

The Night Shift: A Nurse's Tale

Maria had always been drawn to the quiet hum of the hospital. The steady rhythm of machines, the distant beeping of heart monitors, and the muted shuffle of nurses' shoes against the polished linoleum. It was a world of constant motion, yet it somehow managed to feel like time stood still. As a nurse, she had seen it all—the pain, the exhaustion, the miraculous recoveries, and the heartbreaking good-byes. But there were things she couldn't explain, things that stayed with her long after her shifts ended.

It was the night shifts that unsettled her the most. In the dimly lit corridors, the hospital seemed to take on a different life. The usual sounds—voices, footsteps, and laughter—were replaced by an eerie silence that was only broken by the occasional distant cough or the clinking of a cart rolling down the hall. During those long hours, when the hospital was still and quiet, Maria often found herself questioning the things she had witnessed over the years.

There were stories, of course. Stories that floated around the hospital staff like whispers in the wind. Stories of patients seeing things just before they passed away, of shadows that moved when no one was around, and of strange noises that couldn't be explained. Some of her colleagues dismissed them as the byproducts of exhaustion or the mind playing tricks in the stillness of the night. But Maria knew better. She had seen things that no amount of sleep deprivation could explain.

It was on one of those quiet, moonless nights that Maria's encounter with the unknown began. She had just finished checking in on her patients and was making her way down the long, sterile hallways to the supply room. The fluorescent lights flickered above her, casting long shadows on the walls. She paused for a moment, hearing a faint murmur coming from one of the rooms.

At first, she thought it was just a patient calling out in their sleep, but as she walked closer, the voice became clearer. It was soft, almost a whisper, but she could make out the words.

"I can see them... angels... they're waiting for me..."

Maria hesitated at the door, her hand resting on the cool metal handle. She pushed it open slightly, peering inside. The room was dark, with only the soft glow of the heart monitor illuminating the face of the patient in the bed. An elderly man, frail and pale, was lying there, his eyes wide open. His breathing was shallow, and his gaze seemed to be fixed on something that Maria couldn't see.

"Do you see them too?" the man whispered, his voice cracking with age.

Maria stepped into the room, startled. "Who?" she asked, her voice barely above a whisper.

"The angels," he replied, a faint smile tugging at his lips. "They're here to take me home."

Maria's heart raced, and she tried to comfort him. "It's okay, Mr. Daniels," she said gently, taking his hand. "You're not alone."

But Mr. Daniels only smiled and closed his eyes. A moment later, his breathing stopped. Maria's heart dropped as she felt the weight of his passing settle in the room. She had been with him for his final moments, but she couldn't shake the eerie feeling that something beyond the ordinary had just occurred. The mention of angels, the serene look on his face—she couldn't help but wonder if there was more to life and death than what could be explained by science.

As the night wore on, Maria couldn't push the unsettling experience from her mind. She found herself walking the halls with a new sense of awareness, her senses heightened. The quiet hum of the hospital seemed louder now, the stillness more pronounced.

Around 3 a.m., while Maria was checking on another patient, she heard it. A faint tapping sound, like fingers gently drumming against the wall. She looked around, but there was no one in the corridor. She walked to the end of the hall, her footsteps echoing in the silence. The tapping continued, soft at first, then louder.

She reached the nurses' station, where her colleague, Anne, was sitting, filling out some paperwork. "Do you hear that?" Maria asked, her voice shaking slightly.

Anne glanced up from her paperwork and furrowed her brow. "Hear what?"

"The tapping," Maria said, her eyes scanning the empty hallway. "It sounds like someone's knocking on the walls."

Anne chuckled softly. "You're probably just tired. It happens to all of us on the night shift."

Maria didn't respond. She couldn't explain why, but the sound felt wrong. It wasn't just the noise; it was the way it seemed to move, shifting from one spot to another, as if following her down the corridor.

Later that same night, Maria was making her rounds when she saw something in the hallway that made her blood run cold. She had just left the pediatric ward and was walking toward the emergency room when she saw a figure standing at the far end of the hall. It was tall, too tall for any of the patients she had seen in the hospital. At first, she thought it was a nurse or a doctor, but there was something wrong. The figure was shrouded in darkness, its form barely visible in the dim light.

Maria stopped in her tracks, her breath catching in her throat. She blinked, trying to clear her vision, but the figure remained there, unmoving. Her heart began to race, and she felt a cold chill run down her spine.

"Hello?" she called out, her voice trembling.

There was no response. The figure didn't move. It was as if it wasn't even aware of her presence.

Maria took a step forward, her footsteps echoing in the emptiness. But when she looked again, the figure was gone.

She stood there for a long moment, unsure of what she had just seen. Had it been a trick of the light? A shadow cast by one of the hospital's many objects? Or had it been something more?

A few weeks later, Maria encountered another patient who spoke of something similar. Mrs. Greene was an elderly woman who had been in the hospital for several weeks. She had been experiencing heart failure, and her condition was worsening by the day. Maria had grown fond of her—Mrs. Greene was kind and always had a story to tell.

One evening, as Maria was checking on her, Mrs. Greene looked up at her with wide, serious eyes. "I've seen them," she said, her voice trembling. "The angels."

Maria sat down beside her, intrigued but cautious. "What do you mean, Mrs. Greene?"

"I see them when I close my eyes," Mrs. Greene whispered. "They come to me, all glowing and beautiful. They're here to take me home."

Maria felt a shiver run down her spine. The words were too similar to what Mr. Daniels had said. "Do you want me to call anyone for you?" she asked gently, unsure of how to respond.

"No," Mrs. Greene said, smiling softly. "I'm not afraid. They're here for me."

Later that night, Maria returned to check on Mrs. Greene and found her quietly passed away, a peaceful expression on her face. The room was calm, serene, as if she had slipped away into another world. Maria couldn't shake the feeling that there was something more at work—something beyond her understanding.

The final night that would forever change Maria's perspective came without warning. It was a routine shift, one that seemed like any other. The hospital was quiet, and Maria was beginning to feel the exhaustion creep into her bones. She had just finished checking on her last patient of the night when she heard it again—the tapping.

This time, it was louder, more insistent. She followed the sound, her heart racing. As she turned the corner, she saw it—a shadow moving down the hall, just as it had before. But this time, it wasn't alone. There were more shadows—dozens of them—moving silently along the walls, their forms shifting and flickering in the dim light.

Maria stood frozen, her breath shallow and fast. She couldn't move, couldn't speak. It was as if she was trapped in a dream, watching something impossible unfold before her.

And then, a voice—soft, clear, and unmistakable—whispered from the shadows, "You are not alone."

Maria felt the chill of those words sink into her soul. She turned and fled, running back to the nurses' station, her heart pounding in her chest.

She never spoke of the shadows or the whispers again. But from that night on, Maria knew the hospital held more than just the living.

It held the souls of those who had passed, their memories, their whispers, and perhaps even the angels they saw in their final moments.

And every night, as she walked those quiet, lonely halls, she couldn't shake the feeling that she wasn't the only one there.

3

The Last Word

The hospital room was suffused with a quiet, sterile light as Emily sat by her father's side, her hand gently resting in his. The steady beep of the heart monitor was the only sound that filled the room, and with each passing moment, she felt the weight of time bearing down on her. The cancer had taken him slowly, cruelly. At first, it was just a cough, a faint wheeze that Emily chalked up to the stress of work, but within months, they were sitting in sterile doctors' offices, surrounded by medical terminology that seemed foreign and threatening.

Her father, always so strong and full of life, had grown frail. His once booming laugh was now a mere whisper, his tall figure hunched, his energy drained. It was hard for Emily to believe this was the same man who had once carried her on his shoulders through the park, the same man who had taught her how to ride a bike and stayed up with her late into the night, telling her stories of his childhood.

But now, the inevitable was close. She could see it in his eyes—the tiredness, the resignation.

"Dad," Emily whispered, tears welling up. "I love you."

Her father's lips trembled as he tried to speak, but his voice was barely more than a whisper. She leaned in closer, her heart racing.

"Jesus..." he breathed, his eyes meeting hers with a mixture of peace and sorrow. "Jesus..."

It was the last word he ever said. It was strange, almost unsettling at the time—like a prayer, but something deeper, more intimate. A comfort that Emily couldn't understand fully at that moment, but it was a moment that would stay with her forever.

The weeks following her father's death were a blur for Emily. She buried herself in her grief, trying to process the loss of the man who had been her protector, her teacher, and her guiding light. She found herself in the church often, though she didn't quite know why. She wasn't a particularly religious person, but there was something about the quiet of the pews, the peacefulness that seemed to settle over her heart as she sat there.

It was during one of those visits that Emily found herself drawn to the words of a sermon. The preacher spoke of faith, of how even in times of great loss, there was a love greater than any sorrow. She thought about her father's last words—his final breath of "Jesus"—and she felt a stirring deep within her heart. There was something there, something she needed to understand. It was a call, she realized, not just a word.

For the first time, Emily prayed—not the kind of prayer she had grown up with, a prayer that felt like words spoken out of habit, but a real prayer from the heart. She asked for peace. She asked for guidance. And most of all, she asked for understanding.

Emily's journey into Christianity wasn't immediate, but it was steady. She started attending church more regularly, listening to the teachings, reading the Bible, and speaking with others who had found solace in their faith. The more she learned, the more she began to see her father's last words in a new light. Her father had known something. There was a comfort in those words, a reminder that despite everything—despite the pain, the fear, and the uncertainty—there was hope in Jesus.

Her life began to change. She found herself more at peace, more patient, and more understanding. Her heart felt lighter, and even in the midst of daily struggles, she could sense the presence of something greater.

Years passed, and Emily's faith deepened. She graduated from college, where she had initially studied business, unsure of what she wanted to do with her life. But in the years that followed, her path became clearer. She knew she wanted to give back, to make a difference in the lives of others, especially children. It was a natural progression—she had always loved working with children, and her newfound faith made her want to shape the next generation with the values she had come to cherish.

Emily decided to become a teacher. She wanted to create a space where children could not only learn but also experience the love and teachings of Christ. She enrolled in education courses with a focus on early childhood development and began to dream of opening her own Christian kindergarten, a place where children could be nurtured both academically and spiritually.

Five years after that fateful day in her father's hospital room, Emily stood in front of the small, quaint building that would soon house her Christian kindergarten. The paint was fresh, the playground equipment shiny and new, and the door was open, welcoming all who entered. Emily had worked tirelessly to make this dream a reality, and now, as she looked at the building, she felt a surge of pride.

The walls inside were adorned with bright, cheerful images—Bible verses, crosses, and pictures of angels watching over the children. Emily had designed every detail with love, making sure it was a place where children would feel safe, loved, and inspired to grow in their faith.

The first day of school was a mix of excitement and nervousness. As the children and their parents arrived, Emily greeted each one with a warm smile. She could see the apprehension in the parents' eyes, the same way she had felt when she first entered the world of education. But she was ready. She had learned from her own experiences that the most important thing a child needed was love—love for God, love for each other, and love for themselves.

The children were curious and full of energy, their eyes wide with wonder as they entered the classroom. Emily began their first day by reading a story from the Bible, telling them about Jesus' love and kindness. As she spoke, she could see the joy on their faces, and she knew she was doing what she was meant to do.

She was teaching the children the lessons that her father had taught her—lessons of faith, of hope, and of love. And as she watched them play and learn, she couldn't help but smile, knowing that her father's legacy had been passed down through her.

As the months went by, the Christian kindergarten flourished. Emily had hired a small staff, all of whom shared her values and her love for children. Together, they created a warm and nurturing environment where children felt free to explore, to question, and to grow in their faith. Emily incorporated Bible stories into every lesson, teaching the children about kindness, compassion, and forgiveness.

One day, as Emily was reading the story of the Good Samaritan to her class, one of the little boys raised his hand. "Miss Emily," he said, "I want to help people like the man in the story. How can I do that?"

Emily smiled warmly at him. "You can help people every day, just by being kind. It's the little things that matter most. If you see someone who's hurt, or someone who's lonely, you can be their friend. You can show them love."

The boy nodded seriously, taking the lesson to heart. Emily watched him, her heart swelling with pride. She had done it. She had created a space where children could learn not only how to read and write but also how to love and care for others. And it was all rooted in the faith that had carried her through her own life.

Her father's words, "Jesus," still echoed in her heart, reminding her every day of the importance of faith and the legacy he had left her. As she continued her work, she realized that his final words were a gift, a call to something greater than herself, and she was living that call every day.

Years passed, and the kindergarten continued to thrive. Emily's faith only grew stronger, and her desire to help children learn about Jesus and His love deepened. She had become more than just a teacher; she had become a mentor, a guide, and a mother figure to many of the children who passed through her doors.

Looking back on her journey, Emily knew that every step had led her to this point. Her father's death, his final words, and the years of struggle had all been part of a divine plan that had shaped her life. And now, as she watched the children playing in the yard, singing songs of praise, and learning about the love of Jesus, she felt a deep sense of peace.

Her father had always believed in the power of love, of faith, and of family. Emily had taken those lessons to heart and had built something beautiful in his memory—a place where children could experience the love of Christ and learn to live with kindness, compassion, and grace.

4

The Second Chance

Mark sat on the edge of his bed, staring at the gun in his hands. The cold steel seemed to reflect the emptiness he felt deep inside, a hollowness he couldn't shake. His life had felt like it had fallen apart ever since Rachel, his girlfriend of five years, had left him. She had told him she didn't love him anymore, that their relationship had simply run its course. The words hit him like a punch to the stomach, leaving him gasping for air, unable to comprehend how things had changed so quickly.

They had been everything to each other, or so he had believed. But Rachel had decided otherwise, and the pain of losing her was overwhelming. The nights were the hardest, when the silence of the apartment filled every corner. He missed her smile, her laugh, the way she would curl up on the couch with him and talk about their dreams. Now, those dreams felt as empty as the space beside him in the bed.

Mark didn't know how to keep going. His friends and family had tried to offer comfort, but nothing seemed to help. Nothing seemed to matter anymore. The world outside continued to move on, but he felt frozen, stuck in a moment of unbearable sadness.

His father's gun had been in the house for as long as he could remember. It was kept locked up in a safe, a symbol of his father's cautious nature. It was meant for protection, a safety net in case of danger. But now, it seemed to offer Mark a way out of his suffering.

He had always been a responsible man, someone who took care of others. But in this moment, there was no strength left in him to carry on. He didn't want to be a burden, and he didn't want to face a future without Rachel. He pressed the barrel of the gun to his neck, his hand trembling slightly as he took a deep breath.

With a final thought of relief, Mark pulled the trigger.

The sound of the shot was deafening, the force of it knocking him backward onto the floor. He felt an intense pain, a burning sensation spreading through his neck. But then, everything went black.

It felt like an eternity before Mark became aware of his surroundings again. The pain in his neck was excruciating, and he tried to scream but couldn't. Something was terribly wrong. His face felt... different. He reached up to touch it, but it felt as though something was missing. His hands found nothing but smooth, raw skin where his nose and mouth had once been.

Panic set in. He tried to move, but his body felt numb, unresponsive. Was he alive? Had he truly gone through with it?

The door to his bedroom burst open, and his father's voice filled the room. "Mark! What happened? Mark!"

Mark's father had been home when he shot himself. He had heard the gunshot and rushed to his son's room, praying it wasn't what he feared. When he saw his son on the floor, barely conscious, blood dripping from his neck, he immediately called for an ambulance.

The paramedics arrived in a rush, and Mark was quickly rushed to the hospital. It was touch-and-go for a while as doctors worked to stabilize him. The damage to his neck had been severe, and the shock of the injury left him unconscious for several days.

When Mark finally woke up, he was surrounded by beeping machines and the sterile smell of the hospital. His father was sitting beside him, his face pale with worry, but also a quiet relief. "Son," his father whispered, tears in his eyes, "You're still here. Thank God."

Mark tried to speak, but his throat felt raw, and his face... his face felt wrong. He reached up, but still couldn't comprehend what had happened. His nose and mouth were gone, leaving only a mangled, scarred visage. His reflection in the window opposite his bed showed a face that was unrecognizable, and the horror of it made him gasp for breath.

It was the accident. The gunshot. He had almost died, but instead, he was left with a life that now seemed more of a curse than a blessing.

Weeks passed as Mark struggled to come to terms with his new reality. His face had been permanently disfigured, and though his body had healed, the emotional scars ran much deeper. He felt like a stranger in his own skin. His father, devastated by the sight of his son's injury, stayed by his side through the painful recovery process. But no matter how much love and support his family gave him, Mark couldn't shake the feeling of being broken.

Then one day, something miraculous happened.

An article appeared in the newspaper about the accident. It was a brief piece, just a mention of the local man who had tragically attempted suicide and survived. What the article didn't mention was the part of the story that would change Mark's life forever.

Dr. Anthony Hart, a renowned plastic surgeon who had made headlines for his work on facial reconstruction, read the article. He was known for his skill in restoring damaged faces to their former glory. Upon reading about Mark's injury, he felt compelled to help. Dr. Hart had faced many challenges in his career, but this case struck a personal chord with him. The idea of someone feeling so hopeless, so lost, that they would take such a drastic step, resonated deeply.

The doctor reached out to Mark's family and offered to perform the surgery for free. His gift wasn't just in his skill as a surgeon; it was in his deep compassion for others. He wanted to give Mark a second chance, not only to restore his appearance but also to help him find the will to live again.

When Mark underwent the surgery, it was a long and painful process. The damage to his face had been severe, and the reconstruction took months of delicate work. But Dr. Hart's skill was nothing short of miraculous. Over time, Mark's face healed, and although he still carried the scars of his past, the difference was astonishing. His nose and mouth were reconstructed, and while they were not exactly as they had been before, they were close enough to make him look almost the same as he had before the accident.

The transformation wasn't just physical. Mark began to feel a sense of hope slowly returning to him. He had come so close to ending his life, and now, here he was, standing at the threshold of a new beginning. His father, still by his side, couldn't believe how much his son had changed. Mark's eyes no longer held the same despair. There was a quiet strength in them now, a recognition that life, however difficult, was still worth living.

It wasn't an easy road to recovery, but over time, Mark learned to accept his new face and the second chance he had been given. He also began to understand something profound: He was alive for a reason. He had survived for a purpose.

As the years went by, Mark's life took unexpected turns. He never forgot the pain he had felt or the overwhelming darkness that had once consumed him. But he had found a new sense of purpose. He worked through his grief and found peace in helping others. He became an advocate for mental health awareness, speaking out about the importance of seeking help before it was too late. He dedicated himself to helping those who felt as hopeless as he once had.

Mark's second chance at life wasn't just about physical recovery; it was about finding redemption, hope, and love again. His father had saved him, but it was Mark's own strength, and the kindness of those around him, that gave him the courage to rebuild his life.

Mark had come so close to ending it all, but now, as he looked in the mirror, he saw someone who had fought to stay alive — someone who had been given the gift of living. And he wasn't going to waste it.

5

Shadows Behind the Badge

Officer Mark Randall had always believed in justice. Growing up in a modest neighborhood, he had seen his father, also a police officer, don the badge with pride. It symbolized courage, protection, and an unyielding commitment to the community. But as years passed, Mark realized that the weight of the badge wasn't just physical—it came with burdens he could have never foreseen.

Mark joined the force at 22, eager to make a difference. The academy had trained him to handle weapons, pursue suspects, and enforce the law. But nothing had prepared him for the emotional scars that would come with the job.

The first crack in his armor came a year into his service. Mark and his partner, Steve, responded to a domestic violence call in the middle of a quiet suburb. The couple inside had been arguing loudly, and neighbors had called for help. What started as a routine intervention turned into chaos. As Mark stepped into the living room, the man, drunk and enraged, pulled out a gun. Shots rang out, and in the melee, Steve was hit. Mark returned fire, neutralizing the threat, but the sight of his partner bleeding on the floor haunted him for weeks.

Steve survived, but the incident left a shadow over Mark. He began to experience sleepless nights, replaying the event in his mind. He felt guilty for not reacting faster and saving Steve from injury. But there was no time to dwell; the streets demanded his attention, day after day.

Mark buried himself in his work, suppressing his emotions. He convinced himself that if he stayed busy, the memories wouldn't catch up. But the job only got more brutal. Night patrols often dragged him into the darkest corners of the city—gang violence, armed robberies, and the despair of addiction. Each case left its mark.

One evening, Mark responded to a reported break-in at a convenience store. As he entered, he found a teenage boy trembling behind the counter, holding a gun far too big for his hands. The boy was scared, desperate, and Mark tried to de-escalate the situation. "Put the gun down, son. We can talk," Mark said, his voice calm but firm.

The boy hesitated, tears streaking his dirty face. But before Mark could take another step, a commotion erupted outside, and the boy panicked. The gun went off, narrowly missing Mark's shoulder. In a split second, his training kicked in. He fired, and the boy collapsed.

The boy survived, but the incident shattered Mark's resolve. He learned the boy had stolen the gun to protect his siblings from their abusive father. The knowledge gnawed at him. He had acted according to protocol, but the line between right and wrong began to blur in his mind. Was he truly helping, or was he just another cog in a machine that perpetuated pain?

At first, Mark tried to cope with long runs and workouts. But no amount of physical exertion could silence the memories of trembling hands holding a gun or the bloodied face of a young boy. Then came the nightmares. They were relentless, leaving him drenched in sweat, his heart pounding like he was still in the field.

One night, after waking from a particularly vivid nightmare, Mark reached for a bottle of whiskey. "Just one drink to calm my nerves," he told himself. But one turned into two, then three. The warm numbness in his chest was the only escape he could find.

His colleagues began to notice a change. Mark was quieter, often distracted. He brushed off their concerns, saying, "I'm fine, just tired." But the truth was far darker. On top of the alcohol, he started taking prescription medication—a mix of tranquilizers and sleep aids prescribed after he mentioned his insomnia to the department counselor. At first, they helped. But soon, he relied on them just to get through the day.

Mark's lowest point came during a routine traffic stop. A driver had run a red light, and Mark pulled him over. As he approached the vehicle, he felt his chest tighten. His vision blurred, and his breathing became shallow. The world around him seemed to close in, the sounds of the city muffled by the pounding in his ears. He was having a panic attack.

The driver noticed and asked, "Officer, are you okay?" The question felt like a spotlight on Mark's crumbling state. He waved the driver off with a warning and stumbled back to his car, gripping the steering wheel until his knuckles turned white.

That night, Mark sat alone in his dimly lit apartment, staring at his badge on the coffee table. It no longer felt like a symbol of pride—it was a reminder of everything he had endured and the man he was becoming. He thought of his father, who had retired with honor, and wondered if he would ever make it that far.

As the weeks passed, Mark spiraled further. He began isolating himself from friends and family. His sister, Emily, reached out frequently, but he ignored her calls. The department sent him to mandatory counseling sessions, but he treated them as a formality, refusing to open up.

It wasn't until he missed a shift after a night of heavy drinking that the department intervened. His supervisor, Captain Harris, called him into the office. "Mark, we're worried about you," Harris said, his tone firm but compassionate. "You're one of the best officers we have, but I can't ignore what's been happening. You need help."

Reluctantly, Mark agreed to take a leave of absence and enter a rehabilitation program for first responders. The facility was located on the outskirts of the city, surrounded by serene forests and far removed from the chaos of urban life.

At first, Mark resisted the program. Group therapy sessions felt invasive, and he hated the vulnerability of sharing his pain with strangers. But over time, he began to see the value in hearing others' stories. He wasn't alone—many of his fellow officers, firefighters, and paramedics carried similar burdens.

One day, during a private session with his therapist, Dr. Owens, Mark broke down. "I feel like I've lost myself," he admitted, tears streaming down his face. "Every time I close my eyes, I see their faces—the boy, my partner, everyone I couldn't save."

Dr. Owens nodded, her expression gentle. "Mark, you've been carrying these weights alone for too long. It's okay to feel this way. What matters is how you move forward."

As the weeks turned into months, Mark began to heal. He learned techniques to manage his panic attacks and started journaling his experiences—a practice Dr. Owens recommended. Writing allowed him to process his emotions in a way he had never done before.

Slowly, he reconnected with Emily, who had been worried sick about him. "I'm sorry for shutting you out," he told her over coffee one afternoon. She smiled, squeezing his hand. "I'm just glad you're trying, Mark. That's all I ever wanted."

When Mark returned to the force, he was a changed man. He requested a position in community outreach, focusing on mentoring at-risk youth. He saw it as a way to prevent others from making the same mistakes as the boy in the convenience store.

Though the scars of his past remained, Mark no longer let them define him. He had faced the shadows behind the badge and emerged stronger, more compassionate, and ready to make a difference—not just as a cop, but as a human being.

Mark had woken up that morning with a pounding headache and the bitter taste of regret. The empty bottle of rum sat on the kitchen counter like a silent reminder of his growing problem. He knew he shouldn't drive, but his pride refused to let him call in sick again. The thought of facing Captain Harris's disappointment loomed over him like a storm cloud.

"I'll be fine," he muttered to himself, splashing cold water on his face. He popped two aspirin, grabbed his badge, and headed out the door.

The world outside was still waking up, the streets bathed in the soft orange glow of sunrise. Mark climbed into his car, his hands trembling as he gripped the wheel. The dizziness from last night's binge hadn't entirely faded, and his vision blurred slightly as he adjusted his rearview mirror.

The drive to the station started uneventfully, but as Mark approached a busy intersection, his reflexes faltered. A red light appeared ahead, and though he saw it, his sluggish mind delayed his reaction. By the time he slammed on the brakes, it was too late.

A sedan crossing the intersection collided with his car's passenger side, spinning him around. The screech of tires and the crunch of metal echoed in his ears as the world tilted. His car came to a halt on the sidewalk, smoke rising from the crumpled hood.

Mark sat dazed, the airbag pressing against his chest. He could hear shouting outside—bystanders rushing to help—but his head felt like it was underwater. Slowly, he pushed the airbag aside and stumbled out of the car.

The driver of the other vehicle, a middle-aged woman, was already on her phone, presumably calling the police. "Are you okay?" she asked, her voice laced with concern and anger.

Mark nodded numbly, though his knees felt weak. As he leaned against his car for support, the sound of sirens approached.

The responding officers quickly assessed the situation. Mark's badge didn't go unnoticed, but neither did the smell of alcohol on his breath. One of the officers, a young recruit named Daniels, looked at him with a mixture of pity and disappointment.

"Detective Evans," Daniels said cautiously, "have you been drinking?"

Mark hesitated, his mind racing. He considered lying but knew it was pointless. His career had already taken enough hits; adding dishonesty to the mix wouldn't help.

"Yes," he admitted, his voice barely above a whisper. "Last night."

Daniels exchanged a glance with his partner before sighing. "We're going to need to perform a breathalyzer test."

Mark nodded, accepting his fate. The test confirmed what everyone suspected—his blood alcohol level was still over the legal limit from the previous night's drinking.

Back at the station, Captain Harris was waiting for him. The disappointment on Harris's face cut deeper than any reprimand could.

"Mark," he began, his tone heavy, "I've defended you more times than I can count. I've covered for you, made excuses, and given you every chance to turn things around. But this...this is inexcusable."

Mark lowered his head, unable to meet his captain's gaze. "I'm sorry," he said weakly.

"Sorry doesn't cut it," Harris snapped. "You could've killed someone. Do you understand that? You've not only put your career at risk but also the integrity of this department."

Harris sighed deeply, pinching the bridge of his nose. "You're suspended indefinitely. Go home, Mark. And get help—real help this time."

The suspension felt like both a punishment and a lifeline. With no job to distract him, Mark was forced to confront the wreckage of his life. His apartment, once a sanctuary, now felt suffocating. The walls seemed to close in, reminding him of every mistake, every failure.

Emily showed up unannounced one afternoon, her eyes filled with worry. "Mark, you need to stop this before it's too late," she pleaded. "You're my brother, and I love you, but I can't keep watching you destroy yourself."

Her words struck a chord. For the first time, Mark allowed himself to imagine a future where he wasn't drowning in alcohol and regret.

He enrolled in a rigorous rehab program, this time fully committing to the process. The sessions were grueling, forcing him to confront the root of his pain. He shared stories he had kept buried for years—the loss of his partner, the boy in the convenience store, and the constant fear that came with his job.

Through therapy, Mark began to understand that his drinking was a way to numb the overwhelming guilt and anxiety that had consumed him. He learned healthier coping mechanisms and started rebuilding his sense of self.

After months of sobriety and self-reflection, Mark reached out to Captain Harris. "I don't expect to get my job back," he said during their meeting, "but I want you to know that I'm trying to be better. For myself, for the department, and for the people I've let down."

Harris studied him for a moment before nodding. "You've got a long road ahead, Mark. But if you're serious about this, I'll support you. Let's start with desk duty and see where it goes."

Returning to the station was both humbling and therapeutic. Mark wasn't out on the streets anymore, but he found purpose in mentoring younger officers. He shared his story openly, hoping to prevent others from making the same mistakes.

One day, he received an unexpected call from the woman involved in the car accident. "I heard about your recovery," she said. "I just wanted to say I'm glad you're turning things around. We all deserve a second chance."

Her words stayed with him, a reminder that redemption was possible, even for someone who had hit rock bottom.

Over time, Mark began to rebuild his life. The scars of his past remained, but they no longer defined him. He found joy in small victories—reconnecting with Emily, celebrating milestones in his sobriety, and rediscovering the pride he once felt in his badge.

Though his journey was far from over, Mark knew he was on the right path. And for the first time in years, he felt hope—hope for a future where he could truly make a difference, both as an officer and as a man.

Mark's journey toward healing didn't happen overnight, but it began with a profound moment of clarity that changed the course of his life.

One Sunday morning, Emily invited him to her church. "You don't have to stay," she said softly. "Just come with me once. It might help."

Mark hesitated. Church had never been a part of his life. He couldn't remember the last time he'd prayed, and he wasn't sure he believed in anything beyond what he could see and touch. But Emily's persistence, combined with his desperation for something—anything—to make him feel whole again, convinced him to go.

The church was small and unassuming, tucked between a bakery and a bookstore. Inside, sunlight streamed through stained glass windows, casting vibrant colors onto the wooden pews. The air smelled faintly of old books and candles, and a quiet sense of peace hung in the room.

Mark sat beside Emily, feeling out of place. He kept his head down, avoiding eye contact with the friendly faces around him. When the pastor began to speak, Mark expected platitudes, but instead, he heard a story about redemption.

The pastor spoke of a man who had lost everything—his family, his home, his sense of purpose—but found solace in faith. "Sometimes, it takes hitting rock bottom to realize you can't do it alone," the pastor said. "That's when God steps in. He meets you in your pain and carries you forward."

The words struck a nerve. Mark felt a lump in his throat as memories of his darkest moments flooded back. The car accident, the suspension, the nights spent staring at the bottom of a bottle—he had been at rock bottom, and he was still clawing his way out.

For the first time in years, Mark prayed. It wasn't eloquent or polished, just a silent plea: *Help me. I don't know how to do this anymore.*

That moment marked the beginning of Mark's spiritual journey. He started attending church regularly, not because he understood everything but because it gave him a sense of hope he hadn't felt in years. The congregation welcomed him without judgment, offering support and encouragement.

One day, after a particularly moving sermon, Mark stayed behind to speak with the pastor. "I'm struggling," he admitted. "I've done things

I'm not proud of. I've hurt people, and I've hurt myself. I don't know if I can be forgiven."

The pastor smiled gently. "Forgiveness isn't about what you've done; it's about what God has done for you. He offers grace freely. All you have to do is accept it."

Mark felt tears welling up in his eyes. For so long, he had carried the weight of his guilt, believing he didn't deserve redemption. But in that moment, he realized he didn't have to carry it alone.

As his faith grew, Mark began making changes in his life. He realized that alcohol wasn't just a crutch; it was a chain keeping him bound to his pain. With the support of his church community and a Christian counselor, he committed to sobriety.

Giving up alcohol wasn't easy. The cravings came like waves, threatening to pull him under. But every time he felt the urge, he turned to prayer. He found solace in scripture, particularly in verses about strength and perseverance. Philippians 4:13 became his mantra: *"I can do all things through Christ who strengthens me."*

One Sunday, the pastor spoke about the importance of caring for the body as a temple of God. The message resonated with Mark, who had neglected his health for years. That afternoon, he threw away his pack of cigarettes, determined to quit smoking.

The withdrawal symptoms were brutal—headaches, irritability, and sleepless nights—but Mark refused to give in. He started chewing gum and drinking herbal tea to cope with the cravings. He also began focusing on physical fitness, something he hadn't done since his academy days.

Running became his salvation. At first, he could barely jog a block without gasping for breath, but he stuck with it. Every morning, he laced up his sneakers and hit the pavement, the cool morning air filling his lungs.

As the weeks went by, his stamina improved. Running cleared his mind and eased his panic attacks, which had once been a daily torment. The rhythmic sound of his footsteps and the steady pace of his breathing became a form of meditation.

One morning, as he ran through the park near his apartment, Mark noticed the beauty around him in a way he never had before. The golden sunlight filtering through the trees, the birds chirping overhead, the gentle rustle of leaves—it all felt like a gift.

He paused by a small lake, his breath visible in the crisp air. Looking out at the still water, he felt an overwhelming sense of gratitude. For the first time in years, he didn't feel weighed down by his past. He was healing, both physically and spiritually.

Mark's newfound sense of purpose extended to his work. When he returned to the station, he was a changed man. He no longer saw his job as a source of anxiety but as an opportunity to serve others. He volunteered to lead community outreach programs, speaking at schools and youth centers about the dangers of substance abuse and the importance of mental health.

His openness about his struggles inspired others. Younger officers began seeking him out for advice, and his colleagues noticed the transformation in his demeanor. The once-broken man who had stumbled into work after a night of drinking was now a pillar of strength and compassion.

Mark's faith also led him to reconnect with his family. He apologized to Emily for pushing her away during his darkest moments. "You never gave up on me," he said, his voice thick with emotion. "I don't deserve your kindness."

Emily hugged him tightly. "You're my brother, Mark. I'll always be here for you."

Years later, Mark stood in front of his congregation, sharing his testimony during a special service. "I was lost," he said, his voice steady. "I let my pain control me. But God found me in my brokenness and showed me a better way. Through faith, I've learned that redemption is possible for anyone willing to seek it."

The applause that followed was warm and genuine, but Mark didn't need the validation. He already knew the truth: his life had been saved, not just by the grace of God but by his own willingness to change.

Today, Mark's life is far from perfect, but it's real. He starts each day with a run, a prayer, and a sense of purpose. The man who once drowned his sorrows in rum and cigarettes is now a mentor, a brother, and a friend.

And every morning, as he ties his running shoes, he whispers a quiet prayer of thanks—for the second chance he never thought he'd get, and for the faith that carried him through.

6

My childhood's dream

Sophia had always dreamed of becoming a ballerina. From the moment she saw her first performance as a little girl, the pirouettes and elegant leaps etched themselves into her soul. The dancers seemed like ethereal beings, floating effortlessly across the stage. She wanted that too—to live in that magic, to make the world disappear with every graceful movement.

But Sophia's parents didn't see things the same way. They weren't religious, nor did they care much for her dreams. They were practical, focused on achievements, grades, and her future as a doctor or lawyer. "Dreams don't pay the bills," her mother would say, brushing off Sophia's love for dance as childish fantasy.

Her father was stricter. "Top marks, always. Nothing less," he'd bark when her grades faltered even slightly. There was no room for error in their household, no room for distractions. Ballet, they claimed, was a distraction. It was impractical, a waste of time.

Sophia, though, was relentless. She practiced secretly after school, staying late at the studio to perfect her pliés and pirouettes. The late hours and mounting academic pressure soon began to take their toll. Exhaustion became a constant companion, and no matter how hard she tried, she always felt like she was running on empty. Her grades began to slip, and her parents doubled down on their expectations.

One evening, desperate to push through her fatigue, Sophia overheard classmates talking about energy pills. "They're safe," they assured her, "just to keep you focused and awake." Against her better judgment, she decided to try them. At first, they worked like magic. She could study longer, practice harder, and still wake up for another grueling day.

But over time, the pills weren't enough. She began taking more to keep up. Her heart raced, her hands shook, but she ignored the warning signs. She told herself it was worth it—that the ends justified the means. Becoming a ballerina was her destiny, and she would do whatever it took.

One evening, after a particularly grueling day filled with a marathon of studying, practicing, and a steady stream of energy pills, Sophia felt a strange heaviness settling into her chest. The sharp pulse in her temples intensified, but she pushed through. As the night wore on, the weight of the world—of expectations, both hers and her parents'—pressed down on her. Her fingers trembled as she opened another bottle of pills, the white capsules promising to stave off her exhaustion for a few more hours.

She didn't even hesitate. She swallowed them without a second thought. But this time, something went horribly wrong. A dizzying wave of nausea hit her with a force that made her knees buckle. She reached out for the desk, but everything spun. Her vision blurred. She could barely stand as her body swayed, the room around her seeming to distort. Panic seized her, but the pills had already taken their toll. She collapsed to the floor, unable to hold onto consciousness.

In the darkness, Sophia's mind seemed to slip into a void. For a brief moment, she thought she was dead. The overwhelming silence wrapped around her like a heavy blanket. But then, something strange happened. She could feel her body—lying still on the cold floor—but at the same time, she felt like she was floating above it, watching it from a distance. Her heart thudded in her chest as she realized she was no longer just in her body. She was somewhere else. The world around her transformed.

At first, it was hard to describe what she was seeing. Shapes, colors, and energies moved around her in patterns she couldn't quite grasp. Everything was fluid—no longer bound by the laws of nature that had governed her life on Earth. It was as if the entire realm was vibrating with an unseen force. Energy. Everything, from the air to the ground, to the very essence of being, was energy—alive, dynamic, interconnected. Sophia felt it deeply in her bones, like a pulse running through her veins.

In this realm, the very fabric of reality seemed to breathe with life. There were no solid objects, no familiar faces, no clear sky or ground beneath her. Instead, there were swirling energies—seals, like shimmering rings of light, forming intricate patterns in the vast expanse. Each seal seemed to hold a piece of knowledge, a part of the greater truth, a whisper of the universe's secrets. She reached out instinctively, and as her fingers touched one of the seals, the energy resonated through her, filling her with a profound understanding.

She wasn't just in this space. She was a part of it, and it was a part of her. Everything was connected. Every breath, every action, every thought, was a thread in the cosmic web that bound all existence together.

Sophia's heart raced as she began to sense the deeper meaning of her surroundings. She saw flashes of her life—her childhood, her dreams, the years of sacrifice, and the pressure she had endured from her parents. She saw herself as a little girl, dancing with abandon, unburdened by the weight of expectations. But then, the vision shifted.

She saw her adult self, tangled in a web of obligations, trapped by the false belief that she had to prove herself to others. The dreams she had once held so dearly—of dancing, of freedom, of expression—were overshadowed by a relentless need to please others. Her obsession with becoming a ballerina was no longer about the art itself. It had become a desperate attempt to fill the emptiness inside her, to gain validation from her parents and the world. She had sacrificed herself in pursuit of an identity that wasn't even her own.

And in that moment, she realized the truth: she had never truly poured enough energy into what she loved. She had focused all her efforts on fulfilling a purpose that wasn't meant for her—an identity that wasn't hers to claim.

It wasn't about ballet at all. As this realization sank in, a soft, comforting presence surrounded her. She felt a warmth that was unlike anything she had ever known, as though she was being held in the embrace of something much greater than herself. A voice, not a spoken one, but a knowing, filled her mind.

You were not meant to become a ballerina. Your purpose lies elsewhere.

The words were gentle, not condemning, but filled with an undeniable truth. Sophia's energy, her life force, had been misdirected, misplaced in a pursuit that was never her true calling. The path she had walked was paved with good intentions, but it was not the right path for her. It was not a path of freedom, of self-expression, or joy. It had been a path shaped by the expectations of others—the expectations of her parents, society, and even her own insecurities.

Her time in this other realm, surrounded by the flow of energy and the seals of truth, allowed her to see it all clearly. The weight of her choices, the consequences of her actions, were laid bare before her, but she didn't feel shame or regret. Instead, she felt peace, as if the universe was gently guiding her back to herself. This was not the end. It was the beginning.

The presence surrounding her, the voice, continued, *Everything is energy. You are energy. Your life is energy. Your body is energy. Your thoughts, your dreams, your actions—everything you do is a manifestation of this energy. But not all energy is directed properly. When you focus too much on things that are not meant for you, the flow becomes blocked. When you redirect your energy to something that is true to your soul, the flow is restored.*

Sophia felt as though her very being was being rewritten, like the energy within her was shifting, realigning. She saw herself, not as the girl who was trying to become something she was never meant to be, but as the person she was destined to become. And that person, she realized, had always been there, buried under layers of expectation and self-doubt. The journey back to herself wasn't about achieving success on the world's terms. It was about finding harmony within herself, and with the universe.

As the understanding settled within her, the swirling seals and the vast energy of the realm began to dissolve, fading into the distance. Sophia felt herself being gently pulled back, as if she were returning from a long journey. The warmth, the energy, and the truth lingered in her heart, a quiet whisper urging her to live her life in alignment with the real purpose that awaited her.

And just as suddenly as she had left her body, she found herself back—lying on the floor of her room, gasping for air. Her heart pounded in her chest as she struggled to comprehend what had just happened.

The pills had taken her to another realm, to a place where she could see the energy of life, where she could understand the interconnectedness of everything. It was in that place that she had learned the truth about herself—the truth about her purpose. Ballet, as much as she loved it, was never meant to be the center of her life. It was never meant to define her.

She lay there for a long moment, trying to regain her bearings. The dizziness was gone. The anxiety, the fear, the overwhelming pressure—all of it had been lifted, replaced by a strange sense of calm. For the first time in a long time, Sophia felt at peace.

She had seen the truth, and now, it was time to live it.

As Sophia regained her senses, she noticed the quietness that surrounded her. The world felt different now—lighter, almost. There was an unfamiliar stillness within her, like a calm after the storm. She hadn't realized how much weight she'd been carrying until it was gone. The suffocating pressure to meet her parents' expectations, to be someone she wasn't, to always strive for perfection—it had all evaporated, leaving only a quiet sense of self.

Her heart was still racing, but it wasn't from panic. It was from something deeper. Something liberating. She lay on the floor, her arms splayed out beside her, eyes gazing at the ceiling, as though waiting for the world to realign itself in her vision.

She had seen the truth in that other realm. The revelation that ballet, though beautiful, wasn't her true path was unsettling at first, but as the weight of the understanding settled within her, it felt like a light bulb had switched on. For the first time in years, she felt free. She wasn't bound by the pressure to achieve what others had expected of her. She wasn't bound by the ideals of perfection or success. She was free to be herself.

It was then that she realized the next step in her journey: she had to let go. Let go of the medications she had been using to fuel her energy, let go of the belief that her worth was tied to her achievements, and, most importantly, let go of the toxic environment she had built around herself—the one that relied on external validation.

Sophia slowly pushed herself up from the floor, still disoriented but feeling a sense of clarity she hadn't known was possible. She made her way to the bathroom, splashing cold water on her face to wake up fully. The face in the mirror was hers, but it seemed different now, softer. She was no longer the girl who had been chasing perfection. She was someone new.

The following days were a blur of adjustments. She didn't immediately understand what she was supposed to do with this new perspective on life. Her parents still didn't understand. They never would, not fully. They wanted her to return to ballet, to regain the energy she had once had for it, but Sophia knew, deep down, that the path she was meant to walk wasn't paved with pirouettes or arabesques.

She decided to take a step back from everything, to breathe. She let go of her relentless drive to perform. She threw away the pills, leaving behind the quick fixes she had used to numb her exhaustion and pain. And instead of dancing in studios, she began to walk in nature—slowly at first, letting the fresh air fill her lungs, letting the world around her reset her.

One morning, after a long walk through the park, she sat on a bench, watching the sun rise. There, in the quiet beauty of the moment, Sophia realized something she hadn't expected: she had been disconnected from herself for so long. And now, she was learning to reconnect, not to the girl who once wanted to be a ballerina, but to the woman she was becoming.

During those weeks of transition, Sophia began to notice the subtle ways her body was changing. Her anxiety, though still present, was less overwhelming. The panic attacks that had once gripped her with such intensity were fewer. She no longer reached for a bottle of pills when she felt overwhelmed. Instead, she took long walks, practiced deep breathing, and even tried meditation, something she had dismissed in the past.

One day, as she meditated under the shade of an oak tree, a thought entered her mind, clear and undeniable: *I am not defined by what I do, but by who I am.* It was an awakening, a deep inner knowing that she had spent so many years avoiding. She didn't have to be a ballerina to be worthy of love, of respect, or of happiness. She was already enough.

As Sophia began to trust in this newfound peace, her relationships with others also began to change. She reached out to a few close friends, those who had always supported her, even when she felt distant from them. She began to tell them about her experience—the one she had in that other realm. She told them about the seals, the energy, and the profound truth she had come to understand. To her surprise, they listened without judgment. They were curious, but more than that, they were happy for her. They saw the change in her, the calmness that now surrounded her.

Sophia's parents, however, were a different story. Her mother still pushed her to return to ballet, to pursue a career that would bring them pride. But Sophia no longer felt the need to prove herself to them. She gently told her parents that she couldn't return to the dance world—not because she didn't love it, but because she had outgrown it. It wasn't her path, not anymore.

It wasn't an easy conversation. Her mother's face clouded with disappointment, and her father's eyes were filled with confusion. But for the first time, Sophia stood her ground. She explained that she was healing, finding her true self, and that she didn't need to dance to feel fulfilled. It took time, but eventually, her parents began to understand. They didn't fully embrace her decision, but they learned to respect it.

As the months passed, Sophia felt her inner world shift. The more she let go of the toxic influences in her life, the more her true passions began to emerge. She had always been drawn to helping others, to guiding people through difficult times. She had a natural empathy for others who were struggling with their own sense of purpose, their own self-worth. It was then that Sophia realized her calling wasn't in the spotlight of a stage, but in a quieter, more profound way.

One day, while volunteering at a local community center, she met a woman who had recently gone through a difficult divorce. The woman was struggling with depression and self-doubt, and Sophia felt an immediate connection to her. They sat together, talking for hours, sharing their stories. The woman opened up about her own fears and insecurities, and Sophia listened—really listened, in a way she hadn't been able to before.

It was in that moment that Sophia knew what her next step would be. She wanted to help others who were struggling with their own versions of the pressure and expectations she had faced. She wanted to create a space for healing, for people to reconnect with their true selves.

Sophia went on to study counseling and psychology, dedicating herself to learning how to guide others toward their own truth. She opened a small counseling practice where she helped individuals, particularly young women, overcome the struggles she herself had faced. And though she never became a ballerina, she found a new sense of purpose—one that brought her more fulfillment than any performance ever could.

As the years went by, Sophia continued to walk her path with quiet confidence. She had learned that energy, like life itself, flows in mysterious ways. Sometimes, the path we think we should take is not the one that's meant for us. And sometimes, the most profound lessons come from letting go of the life we thought we wanted and embracing the one we were always meant to live.

And in the stillness of her heart, Sophia knew that she was exactly where she needed to be.

As Sophia continued on her journey of self-healing, she found that the more she let go of her past struggles and expectations, the more clarity she gained about life's true meaning. She no longer felt the need to prove herself, no longer felt the weight of her parents' aspirations or society's demands. For the first time in her life, she felt free—not because everything had fallen into place perfectly, but because she had made peace with the fact that life wasn't meant to be perfect. It was meant to be lived. It was meant to be experienced in its raw, imperfect beauty.

In her counseling practice, Sophia began to notice a recurring theme in the people she worked with. Many of them were struggling with the same inner battles she had once faced—the relentless pursuit of external validation, the weight of trying to live up to the expectations of others, the belief that they needed to achieve something monumental in order to feel worthy. As she helped them unpack their stories, Sophia began to realize that the core of these struggles was rooted in a fundamental misunderstanding: the belief that life was about doing, achieving, and impressing. But that wasn't it at all.

She often found herself reflecting on the simple truth that had emerged during her own healing journey: life was about *being*, not *doing*. It was about existing fully in the present moment, embracing what was, rather than constantly chasing what could be. There was no need to measure her worth by the successes she achieved or the roles she played. Her worth, and everyone's worth, was inherent in simply being alive.

One quiet evening, as Sophia sat in her small, cozy apartment overlooking the city, she began to reflect on how far she had come. She wasn't the girl who had dreamed of being a ballerina anymore, nor was she the woman who had been consumed by anxiety and the need for perfection. She was someone entirely different. She was someone who had learned that the meaning of life wasn't about grand accomplishments or accolades—it was about the way we treated others, the love we shared, and the kindness we extended to ourselves and the world around us.

She had come to understand that the true purpose of life wasn't to chase after external achievements, but to live with an open heart and an open mind, to be kind not only to others but to herself. This revelation didn't come overnight. It had taken years of pain, of searching, of questioning, and of growing. But it had finally clicked into place.

Sophia had learned that life was about the everyday moments—the way the sunlight filtered through the trees on her morning walk, the quiet moments shared with friends, the laughter of her clients as they made progress in their healing, the small acts of kindness she witnessed daily, both big and small. Life was about the connections we made with others, the love we gave, and the joy we could find in simply being alive.

As she reflected on this, she thought about her parents. They still didn't fully understand the path she had chosen, but they had softened over time. She no longer fought with them. Instead, she shared with them the lessons she had learned, not with the intention of changing their minds, but simply to help them see the world through her eyes. Her mother had started to see the value in small, quiet moments, too. They didn't have to be big successes or milestones—they could be as simple as sitting down to a meal together and truly appreciating the food, the company, the warmth of the moment.

Sophia's life was no longer defined by her achievements. It was defined by her ability to show up in the world, to be present, and to be kind. She realized that every person she met, every conversation she had, was an opportunity to practice kindness. It wasn't always easy. There were days when she struggled, when the old pressures crept back in, reminding her of what she once thought she had to be. But those days were becoming fewer and fewer.

One afternoon, after finishing a particularly powerful session with a client who had been struggling with her own journey of self-worth, Sophia walked out of her office feeling a deep sense of fulfillment. It wasn't because of any grand achievement, but because she had simply been there for someone—listening, guiding, showing kindness and compassion. It was the simplest form of healing, but it was the most profound.

That evening, as she sat in her living room with a cup of tea, watching the sunset paint the sky in shades of pink and orange, Sophia found herself thinking back to her experience in that other realm. She thought of the seals, the flowing energy that connected everything in the universe, and how she had learned that life wasn't about forcing things into being, but about letting them flow naturally. Life wasn't meant to be a struggle. It was meant to be a journey—a journey of discovery, of love, and of learning to be present in every moment.

She realized that her journey had come full circle. She no longer needed to be perfect, to prove herself, or to chase some external goal. The meaning of life, as she had come to understand it, was simple: it was about being kind to others and to oneself. It was about living in harmony with the world around her, embracing each moment as it came, and knowing that everything was connected.

And so, as she continued her work, as she continued to live, Sophia found peace in the quiet moments. She no longer searched for meaning in external achievements or the approval of others. She had found it within herself—the simple truth that life was about love, kindness, and being fully present. The pressure to be someone she wasn't had dissipated, and in its place was a sense of calm and contentment that she had never known before.

Sophia knew now that she didn't need to be anything other than what she already was—a person capable of love, of kindness, and of living a life that was truly her own.

7

The Heart's Awakening

Lena had always lived a life filled with ambition. She worked tirelessly in her corporate job, striving for success, meeting deadlines, and chasing after the approval of others. For years, she had been driven by the idea that her worth was tied to her achievements and the way others saw her. But in the past few weeks, something had begun to change.

It started with a dull, persistent ache in her chest. At first, it was nothing more than a slight discomfort, something she could ignore between meetings and emails. But as the days passed, the pain grew sharper, as though something deep inside her heart was trying to break free. She brushed it off, thinking it was stress from work or perhaps a sign of aging. But soon, the discomfort was no longer something she could dismiss.

One evening, as she sat at her desk, the familiar ache returned, but this time it was more intense. She pressed her palm against her chest, trying to soothe the sharp pain. The room felt colder, and the light in the room flickered. Lena's breath became shallow, and a strange sensation washed over her as though the very air around her had shifted.

Suddenly, the pain seemed to surge, and Lena gasped for breath. She stumbled from her chair, clutching her chest, as she fell to her knees. The world around her seemed to blur, her vision narrowing. Her heart raced as if it were trying to escape from her chest. Desperately, she tried to reach for her phone to call for help, but her hands trembled, unable to hold it steady.

In the midst of the growing chaos, a voice, soft and gentle, filled her mind.

"Lena, you are not your body," the voice said, soothing yet commanding. "You are not your mind. You are part of the source."

Lena's eyes widened as she looked around the room. The air grew thick, almost charged with energy. The walls seemed to fade away, and before her appeared a glowing figure, radiating warmth and light. It was an angel—she could feel its presence, peaceful and full of compassion.

The angel stood before her, its eyes filled with understanding. "The pain in your chest is not just physical, Lena. It is a reflection of something deeper, something within your soul that has been ignored for too long."

Lena opened her mouth to speak, but no words came. Instead, she found herself drawn to the angel's presence, a sense of peace and love washing over her. She felt safe, as though she were being cradled in a divine embrace.

"You are not your body, Lena," the angel repeated, its voice soft but firm. "This body, this mind, these thoughts—they are temporary. You are infinite, eternal, a part of the source of all creation."

Lena's heart pounded as she tried to understand. What did the angel mean? She had always thought of herself as her body, her thoughts, her feelings. She had lived her life as if everything was bound by the limits of the physical world.

"Who are you?" Lena whispered, her voice barely a whisper.

"I am an extension of the source," the angel replied, its wings shimmering with light. "I am here to help you remember who you truly are."

As Lena's eyes fell upon the angel, she felt a pull, a gentle invitation to step beyond her body. It was as if the very fabric of her being was being called to transcend the physical realm. The angel's words echoed in her mind: *You are part of the source.*

And then, without any hesitation, Lena felt herself lifting, her body no longer bound by the weight of gravity. She was floating, her consciousness expanding beyond the confines of her skin, her mind opening up to something vast and infinite.

The pain in her chest faded away, replaced by a sense of deep peace. She could feel her body, but it was no longer the same. She was no longer just the person she had been before—the woman driven by ambition, by fear, by the pressures of life. She was something more. She was connected to everything, to the very source of all creation.

The angel's presence remained beside her, a constant source of guidance and love. "Lena," the angel said softly, "this is your true nature. You are not limited by your body, by time, or by your mind. You are part of the divine source, and it is only through letting go of your attachment to your body and your thoughts that you will truly be free."

For the first time in her life, Lena understood. She had been living as if her worth was tied to the success of her career, her physical appearance, and the expectations of others. But those things were fleeting. They were not who she truly was.

"I've been so afraid," Lena whispered, her voice trembling with emotion. "Afraid of losing control, afraid of not being enough."

The angel's light grew brighter, and Lena felt a wave of love wash over her, comforting and soothing her like nothing she had ever known. "Fear is born from attachment," the angel explained. "When you let go of the need to control everything and surrender to the truth of who you are, fear will dissolve. You are whole. You are loved."

As Lena floated in this new realm, her consciousness expanding further, she could see connections everywhere—connections between people, between the stars, between the very atoms of existence. Everything was energy. Everything was interconnected. And everything was a reflection of the divine source.

The pain she had felt in her heart, which she had thought was a sign of something wrong with her, had actually been a wake-up call. It was a signal that she had been disconnected from her true self. She had been living in a way that ignored her soul's deepest desires.

"You are part of the source, Lena," the angel repeated, "and all of creation is within you. You are not separate. You are one with the divine."

Lena closed her eyes, allowing the profound truth to sink in. She felt an overwhelming sense of love and acceptance. She no longer needed to strive for validation or success. She didn't need to push herself to be someone she was not. She was enough, just as she was.

For what seemed like an eternity, Lena floated in the vastness of this divine realm. She saw colors beyond what her earthly eyes could comprehend, and felt emotions that transcended anything she had ever experienced. She realized that this was her true home—the place where she was whole, where she was free from the limitations of her body and mind.

And then, as gently as she had been lifted, Lena began to feel herself returning to her body. She could sense the weight of her physical form again, but this time, it didn't feel as heavy. She was still connected to the source, still a part of something greater. The pain in her chest had completely vanished, replaced by an indescribable peace.

The angel's presence lingered with her, a comforting reminder that she was never alone. "Remember, Lena," the angel said, "you are not your body. You are not your mind. You are part of the source. And in that knowing, you are free."

Lena opened her eyes, now fully aware of her body once again, but with a profound sense of peace. The world around her looked the same, but she was different. She had been awakened to the truth of who she was.

And for the first time in her life, Lena felt truly alive.

As Lena sat quietly in her room, reflecting on the strange, peaceful experience she had just undergone, her thoughts drifted back to her childhood—those years when she was still trying to figure out who she was, when she was overwhelmed by a world that seemed too big and too loud. She thought about the girl she used to be, the one who felt out of place in everything.

Lena had always been an introvert. From a very young age, she preferred to spend time on her own. While other children ran around the playground laughing and playing, Lena would be sitting under a tree, sketching pictures in her notebook or staring off into the distance, lost in her thoughts. She loved art more than anything—creating was her escape from the noise of the world. She felt as though in the strokes of her pencil, in the splash of paint on a canvas, she could express the emotions she struggled to put into words.

But her love for art, for quiet, for stillness, made her different. And that difference made her a target. In a world that celebrated loudness and extroversion, Lena became a target for teasing, bullying, and exclusion.

She could still remember the sharp, taunting voices of her classmates echoing in her mind, like a dull, painful reminder. They would call her names, laugh at her for not fitting in, for not being like the others. "Why are you so weird, Lena?" they would ask. "Why don't you talk to anyone? You're such a freak."

The words stung. They always did. Every day, she walked into school with the fear of being judged, of being ignored or laughed at. Her classmates' cruel words became a constant companion, echoing in the back of her mind, like an incessant drumbeat she couldn't escape. They buried her with their ridicule, with their constant need to push her down, to make her feel like she was not enough.

Her teachers never seemed to notice. No one ever came to her defense. So, Lena learned to live with it. She learned to hide her emotions, to keep her head down, to blend into the background and avoid the spotlight. She was quiet, shy, and awkward, and it seemed as if that was all she would ever be.

At home, things weren't much different. Her parents, though loving, were busy with their own lives. They didn't fully understand what Lena was going through. Her mother would often tell her to be more confident, to stop being so shy, as if it were something she could control. "You need to talk more, Lena," her mother would say, "you can't always be hiding in your room with your drawings. Get out there, make friends. Life is about connections."

But Lena wasn't like that. She didn't want to make friends in the way her mother imagined. She didn't need to fit into a mold that wasn't hers. What she needed was to be accepted for who she was—to be loved without having to change who she was at her core. But her parents didn't see that. They couldn't see past the quiet, the introversion, the shyness.

So, Lena learned to keep her feelings to herself. She kept her pain hidden, locking it away inside where no one could see it. But every day, as she walked home from school, the weight of the world pressed down on her. Every step felt heavier. And often, as she walked the long road home, tears would start to well up in her eyes, unnoticed by the people passing by. The loneliness of it all consumed her, and she would cry as she walked, her sobs muffled by the rush of wind in her ears.

She wondered why she couldn't be like the other girls—outgoing, popular, and confident. Why couldn't she just smile and talk easily, like they did? But no matter how hard she tried, she couldn't change the way she was. She was trapped in a world that didn't seem to have space for someone like her.

The only place where she felt at peace, the only place where she didn't feel like an outsider, was when she was alone with her art. When she was creating, she felt whole, like she was tapping into something deeper within herself, something pure and beautiful. But the world didn't understand that. It didn't understand her need for quiet, her need to be alone with her thoughts, her need to express herself in a way that didn't require words.

And so, she suffered in silence, carrying the pain of rejection and isolation with her every day. But as much as the pain hurt, Lena didn't know how to change. She didn't know how to fix the broken pieces inside her.

One afternoon, after yet another cruel remark from a group of girls in her class, Lena had had enough. She couldn't bear it anymore. She couldn't take the constant feeling of being unwanted, unseen, and misunderstood. As she walked home that day, her heart heavy with despair, she made a vow to herself that she would never let anyone see her hurt again. She would bury her emotions, hide them away where no one could touch them. And so, she did.

From that day forward, Lena kept her pain locked away. She forced herself to go through the motions, to smile when necessary, to pretend like everything was fine. She continued to draw, continued to create, but the joy she once found in it slowly began to fade. Her art became a mask, a way to hide the emptiness she felt inside.

The years went by, and as Lena grew older, the pain of her childhood never truly left her. It became a part of her, like an invisible scar that marked her heart. The sense of being misunderstood, of never truly fitting in, lingered. She pushed those feelings aside, pretending they didn't matter, but deep down, they still hurt.

And now, sitting in her room, reflecting on the angel's message and the journey she had just begun, Lena realized something she had never understood before. The pain she had felt, the rejection, the isolation—it was all a part of her journey. She had spent so many years focusing on her weaknesses, on the parts of herself she thought were wrong or broken. But now, in the light of the angel's wisdom, she could see that those experiences, those struggles, had shaped her into who she was today.

The feelings of loneliness and rejection had been her teachers, guiding her to this moment of understanding. They had shown her that the world didn't need to accept her in order for her to be whole. The approval of others was not what defined her.

Lena wasn't just a quiet, introverted girl anymore. She was so much more. She was a soul on a journey, a being of light and energy, part of the source of all creation. And for the first time, she understood that the pain she had carried for so long was not a curse—it was a gift. A gift that had led her to the truth of who she really was.

And so, as Lena sat quietly in her room, she made a promise to herself: she would no longer hide from her past. She would no longer let the pain of her childhood define her. She was not her body, not her mind, not her past. She was part of the source. And in that knowing, she was free.

8

A Journey to the Light

Ella had always been a curious soul. She loved to learn, always questioning the world around her. Raised in a small town, she found solace in books and the vast knowledge they contained. She was quiet and introspective, often retreating to the safety of her thoughts rather than engaging in social gatherings. Her teachers had always praised her intelligence, but her inner world, filled with questions and doubts, often felt like a place where she could never fully connect with anyone.

One afternoon, during her final year of school, a heated argument broke out in class. It started innocuously enough, with the teacher discussing the creation of the world. He spoke passionately about God being the Creator, the one who designed and shaped everything in existence. Ella, however, could not remain silent. Her mind was too full of questions, of contradictions, of things she didn't quite understand.

"How can anyone claim to know the truth about God?" she had retorted, her voice rising in frustration. "There's no evidence. The world could have evolved without any divine being. Science explains everything."

The teacher looked at her, a hint of sadness in his eyes, but he didn't respond aggressively. "Faith isn't about evidence. It's about belief. It's about trusting in something greater than yourself."

But Ella wasn't ready to accept that. She wasn't a believer. Her worldview was grounded in logic and science, and she couldn't see a place for faith in the world she was trying to understand.

The argument ended with tension in the air, and Ella left the classroom feeling unsettled. She had always felt different from her peers, and this argument had only confirmed her sense of isolation. It was easier to believe in the tangible world, in the physical, the measurable, the explainable. God, faith, and belief in something unseen felt too abstract, too intangible for her.

After graduation, Ella left her small town for the bright lights of the city. The city was full of possibilities, of people who could teach her new things and experiences that could shape her. But the reality of city life wasn't as glamorous as she had imagined. She found herself living in a small apartment in a part of the city that wasn't exactly thriving. She worked at an office job she didn't care about, and soon enough, the loneliness crept in. She had no friends, no connections, and the bustling streets outside only seemed to make her feel more invisible.

At first, Ella tried to fill the void with work, but the stress quickly wore her down. She began to feel an ever-present weight in her chest, a constant anxiety that she couldn't escape. The panic attacks became frequent, coming at unexpected moments, leaving her feeling breathless and paralyzed. The more she tried to fight them, the worse they became. She needed something to calm the overwhelming storm inside her.

One night, after a particularly difficult day at work, Ella met a colleague named Jessica. Jessica was confident, outgoing, and a regular at the city's nightclubs. She invited Ella to join her for a night out, promising that it would be a fun way to blow off steam. Ella hesitated at first, but the thought of being around other people, of escaping the weight of her anxiety, was too tempting to resist. She agreed.

That night, the music in the club was loud, pulsing, almost deafening. Lights flashed, and the air smelled of perfume and sweat. Ella felt alive for the first time in a while, the beat of the music syncing with the rhythm of her heart. Jessica handed her a small bag and a rolled-up bill.

"Just a little boost," Jessica said with a wink, handing Ella some white powder. "It'll help you feel more at ease. You'll be able to enjoy yourself."

Ella wasn't sure. She had never done drugs before. But the anxiety gnawing at her insides made her take the plunge. She snorted a line, then another. At first, she felt a rush—an overwhelming sense of euphoria and relief. The panic attacks seemed miles away, and for once, she felt like she could breathe, like she belonged.

The next few weeks followed a similar pattern. She started using more and more, needing the drug to get through the day. The nights in the club became routine, and every time she felt the anxiety creeping in, she turned to the cocaine to numb it. It became her crutch, the only way she could feel good about herself, the only way she could quiet her thoughts.

But one night, Ella pushed it too far. She was at a party with Jessica, and the urge to escape her reality was stronger than ever. She snorted more than usual, not realizing how much she had taken. It wasn't until she began to feel dizzy and disoriented that she realized something was wrong. The room spun around her, and she stumbled toward the bathroom.

She collapsed onto the cold, tiled floor. Everything felt like it was closing in. The air around her seemed to thicken, and she could hear her heart pounding in her ears. The lights in the bathroom flickered as if they were fading in and out of existence. A dark tunnel began to form in front of her, pulling her in. The coldness of the floor beneath her felt so distant now, as though it no longer mattered. Her body felt weightless, like she was drifting.

In the tunnel, everything shifted. The darkness was replaced by an overwhelming orange hue, like a fiery sunset stretching into the vastness of space. She could see galaxies swirling, stars twinkling with energy, and everything seemed interconnected, as if the universe itself was alive and breathing.

For the first time in her life, Ella felt truly alive, but in a way she couldn't understand. She could feel the energy of everything around her, the connection between her, the stars, the galaxies. It was as if the boundaries of her body didn't matter anymore, and she was part of something far greater, far more profound.

A voice, soft and distant, spoke to her from the depths of the orange glow.

"You are not your body, Ella. You are not your mind. You are part of the Source, part of the energy that flows through everything. The world you see is just a small fragment of the vastness of existence. You are connected to it all."

Ella didn't understand at first. She couldn't comprehend what was happening, but the voice felt like a comforting presence, like a whisper in the dark that soothed her troubled soul. The panic, the anxiety, the fear—all of it seemed insignificant in this vast, infinite realm. She wasn't alone. She was part of something greater than herself.

The next thing Ella knew, she was back in the bathroom, her body aching from the fall. Her vision blurred, and she struggled to breathe. She had narrowly escaped death, but she had also seen something beyond this world, something that made her realize how small her worries really were.

In the days that followed, Ella began to understand what had happened. The drugs hadn't just been a way to numb her pain—they had opened a door, a gateway to a deeper understanding of herself and the universe. She wasn't sure what to believe, but she couldn't ignore the feeling of connection, of purpose, that she had experienced in that dark, orange tunnel.

Ella knew that she had been given a second chance. A chance to change. A chance to find meaning in her life beyond the distractions of the city, the parties, and the drugs. She realized that she was not meant to live a life of escapism, but one of growth, understanding, and healing.

From that day on, Ella began to take steps to heal herself. She sought help for her addiction, started therapy, and began to focus on her inner world. She rediscovered her love for art, using it as a way to express the energy she felt from the universe.

And with time, Ella found peace—peace that came not from escaping her reality, but from embracing the truth that she was a part of something far greater.

9

____

Title: A Dream of Peace

Mike had always been a quiet and calm boy. He wasn't the type to stand out in a crowd or draw attention to himself, and in the rough halls of high school, that meant he was an easy target. It wasn't that he wanted to be left alone—it was just how he was wired. When the other boys laughed, Mike just stood by, watching with his soft brown eyes, wishing things could be different. But that quietness, the way he never stood up for himself, made him a victim. The bullying started small—shoves in the hallway, whispers behind his back. But it grew, and soon, he couldn't walk down the hall without feeling eyes on him.

At home, Mike's father, a stern army man, made it clear that there was no room for weakness in their household. His father believed in discipline, order, and respect. Every night, after school, Mike was expected to work out, to run, to be in the best shape possible. His father believed that strength wasn't just about muscles—it was about mind, spirit, and perseverance. He'd watch Mike lift weights, sometimes with an approving nod, other times with a stern, silent gaze. It wasn't about enjoying the process. It was about the pursuit of being good enough for a father who had high expectations.

But those expectations felt like a weight around Mike's neck, one he could never seem to shake off. He always worked hard, always pushed himself, hoping that one day his father would say, "I'm proud of you," but those words never came. Instead, Mike's life was filled with rigid routines, as if his existence was built upon the idea of constant improvement—a never-ending cycle of self-discipline and self-criticism.

After high school, Mike enlisted in the army, following in his father's footsteps. The army was his chance to prove himself, not just to his father, but to himself. He rose through the ranks, earned respect from his comrades, and even became a respected leader. But the truth was, no matter how many battles he won, how many promotions he earned, a quiet emptiness lingered. His father's voice, always in his head, pushed him to be better, but it was never enough. There was always more to achieve, more to prove.

Then came the phone call that shattered his world. His father had passed away suddenly, the man who had been the constant force in his life, the man whose approval Mike had spent his entire life seeking, was gone. Mike hadn't been prepared. He wasn't ready to face a life without the only person who had shaped him into the man he had become. The weight that had burdened him for so long—trying to be the best, trying to earn the approval that seemed always out of reach—was now gone. And with it, Mike felt completely adrift.

For the first time in years, he let himself rest. He let go of his workouts, his routines, and fell into a depression that wrapped itself around him like a thick, suffocating blanket. He stopped exercising, stopped pushing himself, and all those dreams of ever being good enough faded away. There was no point anymore. No purpose. He was alone, and the silence felt louder than the noise of the world he had once inhabited.

But then, something unexpected started to happen. Every time Mike closed his eyes to sleep, he found himself in a dream—a place where the world seemed different, almost ethereal, where everything felt peaceful and warm. At first, he thought it was just his mind trying to escape from the harsh reality of his loss. But the dreams kept coming, night after night. He found himself sitting at a dinner table in a cozy, softly lit room. Across from him was his father, just as he had been before, with the same stern yet loving eyes. There was no judgment in his gaze, only warmth, a quiet understanding.

"Come, join me," his father would say, smiling in the way Mike had always wanted to see. And for a moment, Mike would forget about the pain. He would forget about the long years of trying to prove himself. In those dreams, there was no judgment, no expectations—only acceptance. But then, just as he would reach out, just as he would take a seat at the table, he would wake up. The dream would dissolve, leaving him with a feeling of longing, of emptiness.

He couldn't explain it, but somehow, it felt as though his father was still with him, even in death. There was a comfort in those dreams, an almost spiritual presence that he couldn't quite understand. In the darkness of the night, as he lay in his bed, his mind would wander back to those dinners, to the soft smile on his father's face, and the words he never thought he'd hear.

It wasn't just his father he saw, though. In the dreams, there was a presence of something greater, something that felt almost divine. The energy of the dreams was different—bright, warm, and unexplainable. Mike began to wonder if there was more to life than just the physical world. He had always dismissed the idea of spirituality, dismissing it as something for the weak or those unable to face reality. But now, he wasn't so sure.

One night, after a particularly vivid dream in which his father had invited him once again to sit at the dinner table, Mike woke with a new sense of clarity. His father's absence still left a hole in his heart, but in the midst of that emptiness, there was also a new understanding. His father had been harsh at times, demanding, always pushing Mike to be more, to be better. But in the end, Mike realized, it wasn't about the pursuit of perfection. It wasn't about being the best in the world or even in his father's eyes. It was about love. His father had loved him in his own way, but more than that, life was about connection, not perfection.

Mike began to look at life differently. The dreams with his father became more frequent, and each time, they brought him closer to peace. He began to work on healing the parts of himself he had neglected for so long—the parts that needed love and kindness, not discipline and harshness. Slowly, he started to exercise again, but this time it wasn't out of obligation or the need to prove something to someone. It was because it made him feel good, because it helped him reconnect with his body and his mind. It was the beginning of healing.

And as Mike continued to dream, as he continued to find peace in the presence of his father and the love he had longed for, he realized that the greatest gift he could give himself wasn't being the best at anything—it was simply to allow himself to be. To be loved, to feel peace, and to understand that sometimes, even when we don't get what we think we want, life has a way of guiding us to where we need to be.

As a young man, Mike had felt an unwavering pull toward the army. It wasn't just a career path—it was a way to honor his father, the man whose expectations had shaped his life, whose legacy Mike had carried with him, whether he realized it or not. The army was a place where discipline, order, and resilience were revered. It was a place where Mike could feel connected to his father's spirit, even though his father was no longer around to see him.

Mike enlisted right after high school, a decision that seemed to fulfill his need for structure, for purpose. The rigid routines of boot camp had been challenging, but Mike thrived in them. He rose through the ranks, becoming a respected figure among his peers, though he always remained quiet and calm, never one to boast or seek attention. Deep inside, however, he still battled with the need for approval that had been instilled in him during his childhood.

But something unexpected happened in the midst of his service. Mike met Rachel.

She was a gentle soul, soft-spoken yet confident, with a quiet strength that drew Mike in. They met at a military event, and there was an immediate connection, one that transcended the usual camaraderie between soldiers. Rachel saw through Mike's tough exterior. She understood the vulnerability behind the stoic soldier. She could tell that Mike wasn't just looking for honor or approval from others—he was looking for a place where he could truly belong.

Their connection grew over time. They spent quiet evenings together, talking about their dreams and their fears. Rachel would often speak of her own struggles, and Mike would listen—really listen, in a way that made her feel heard. Slowly, they fell in love. It wasn't a whirlwind romance, but something deeper, more profound. Rachel understood Mike in ways no one ever had. She was the kind of woman who saw beauty in the quiet moments and believed in the strength of love to heal all wounds.

A year later, they were blessed with a baby girl, Emma. She was everything they had hoped for and more. Mike, who had spent so many years focusing on being the best soldier he could be, now found himself holding his daughter in his arms, overwhelmed with love. He could see the promise of a future that was brighter than the one he had known—a future built on the love and joy that Rachel and Emma had brought into his life.

But the peace that Mike had found with his family was short-lived. He was deployed on a mission to a desert region, where the heat was unbearable and the terrain unforgiving. The mission was meant to be routine—nothing too dangerous. But that changed in an instant.

Mike was walking through the dusty, barren landscape, scanning for threats, when he stepped on something he couldn't see. The explosion sent him flying through the air, his body crashing to the ground with a violent force. His leg had been torn apart by the blast. Mike screamed in agony as the world around him blurred into a haze. He felt himself losing consciousness, the pain too intense to bear.

And then, something strange happened.

In that moment of pain and confusion, Mike felt himself leave his body. It was as though he was hovering above it, detached from the pain, observing his broken form from a distance. The world around him grew quiet, and he began to drift, floating in a dark, endless space. The colors were muted, the air thick with an unsettling silence. Mike wasn't sure where he was or what was happening.

But then, a vision appeared. He was now watching scenes unfold—scenes of his past. He saw himself as a child, the quiet boy who had been bullied, the one who had lived under the constant pressure to meet his father's high expectations. He saw himself in the army, fighting battles, but also pushing others too hard, using his discipline as a weapon rather than a tool for growth. He saw his own words, harsh and unforgiving, spoken to those who had only tried to help him. He saw the times when he had been selfish, when he had placed his own needs above the well-being of others.

It was painful to watch, the shame and regret rising within him like a tide. The visions kept coming, one after another—times when he had failed others, when he had hurt them without even realizing the impact of his actions. The weight of it all was crushing. Mike wanted to turn away, to escape the suffocating guilt, but he couldn't. He was trapped in this reflection of his own choice.

Time seemed to stretch on forever in this space. What felt like years passed in what could have only been moments. Mike felt as though he was trapped in a never-ending loop of his own regrets. But just as he thought he couldn't bear it any longer, something changed.

A warmth began to spread through him. It started in his chest, like a soft, golden light. It grew brighter, warmer, and soon it enveloped his entire being. The guilt, the pain, the weight of his regrets—all of it started to lift, replaced by a sense of peace and love. The golden light was like a blanket, wrapping him in comfort, a warmth so pure that it soothed every corner of his being. The fear and sorrow he had carried with him for so long seemed to melt away, replaced by an overwhelming sense of compassion and understanding.

And then, a figure appeared before him. It was a man, radiating golden light, his presence calm and serene. Mike felt a sense of recognition, but he wasn't sure why. The man's face was kind, full of love, and his eyes held an ancient wisdom that Mike couldn't quite comprehend.

The figure spoke in a gentle, soothing voice. "Do not be afraid. You are not alone, and you are not defined by your past actions. The light you feel is not a punishment—it is a gift. You are being shown the path to healing."

Mike, still floating in the golden light, asked, "Are you Jesus?"

The man smiled softly, a knowing look in his eyes. "No, I am not him. But I am here to guide you. I am here to help you understand the truth about yourself. You are not your past. You are not the mistakes you've made. You are a being of light, just like everything around you."

Mike listened, confused but comforted. "But I've done so many things wrong. How can I be a being of light?"

The man's expression remained calm, filled with a love that Mike couldn't fully understand. "Every being has a purpose. And every being has the ability to heal and grow. You have always been yourself, Mike. The key to healing is accepting that you are enough as you are, in all your flaws and all your beauty. The love you seek begins within you. It is not something to be earned or found outside of yourself—it is something to be nurtured and shared. And in that love, you will find the strength to forgive yourself."

Mike felt the weight of the man's words, his heart opening to a truth he had never fully understood before. The golden light continued to surround him, and for the first time in his life, he felt at peace—truly at peace.

"You must learn to be yourself," the man continued. "Only then will you be able to create the energy of love that will guide you through this world. It is not about being perfect or living up to the expectations of others. It is about accepting who you are and using that acceptance to build a life of love and compassion."

As the man spoke, Mike felt his body being filled with warmth and peace. It was as though every cell in his body was being recharged with the purest form of energy—a love that transcended everything he had known. He felt his mind clearing, his heart softening. And in that moment, Mike understood. His life wasn't about pleasing others, earning approval, or proving anything. It was about love. It was about being kind, not only to others but to himself.

With those final words, the golden light grew even brighter, and Mike felt himself drifting back toward his body. The warmth, the love, the peace all seemed to remain with him as he awoke, blinking in the harsh light of the hospital room. His leg was gone, but the sense of peace that had filled him remained.

And for the first time, Mike understood that the journey he had been on—the pain, the loss, the struggle—had all led him to this moment of awakening. He wasn't just a soldier. He wasn't just a son or a father. He was a soul, and in that soul, there was infinite potential for love and healing.

And as he lay in his hospital bed, Mike smiled softly, knowing that he was no longer alone. He had found the light within himself, and that light would guide him forward into the next chapter of his life.

Mike's mind was a whirlwind as he lay in the sterile hospital room, the steady beeping of the machines around him the only sound breaking through the silence. His leg was gone, and a part of him felt like he had lost more than just a limb. His thoughts lingered on Rachel, his wife.

She hadn't come to see him. Not once.

His heart ached, a different kind of pain that cut deeper than the physical injuries he had sustained in the explosion. Mike had always been a man of strength, a man who could face adversity head-on, but this—this was something he couldn't quite conquer. In the days following the attack, his recovery had been slow, and with each passing moment, the reality of his situation began to set in. But it wasn't just the loss of his leg that hurt; it was the silence. The absence of Rachel.

His phone, which had been placed on the bedside table, vibrated, its harsh tone interrupting the endless, painful quiet. He hesitated for a moment, before reaching for it with his remaining hand. The screen flashed with an unfamiliar name, and Mike's heart sank. He didn't want to look, but he couldn't resist.

It was a message from a mutual friend, someone who had known Rachel for years. Mike's eyes scanned the text, each word piercing his soul. "Mike, I'm sorry to tell you this, but Rachel's been seeing someone else. She's with another man now. She didn't want you to find out this way."

The words blurred before his eyes. He felt a wave of shock followed by an overwhelming sense of betrayal. Rachel—the woman he had loved, the woman who had been his world—had moved on so quickly. The woman who had promised him she would be there, no matter what, was now with someone else.

His mind raced, and a flood of emotions threatened to drown him. Anger. Grief. Confusion. There was no clarity, only a storm of feelings that he didn't know how to navigate. His heart hurt, but it wasn't just from the physical pain. It was the hollow emptiness that came from the betrayal of someone he had trusted with everything.

Days turned into weeks, and the hospital room became both a refuge and a prison. He had no visitors. No messages from Rachel. No sign that she cared. The space around him felt suffocating, and the sense of abandonment grew heavier with each passing day. It felt as though the life he had once known had slipped away from him, leaving him adrift in an ocean of uncertainty.

But even amidst the pain, Mike couldn't shake the lessons he had learned in his brief, otherworldly experience. The vision of the golden light, the soothing presence of the guide, the love that had filled him during that fleeting moment—those feelings hadn't disappeared. They still lingered deep within him, like a flicker of hope, a reminder that there was more to life than the suffering he was experiencing.

One night, as he lay staring at the ceiling, Mike made a decision. He had spent years living for others—seeking his father's approval, meeting the expectations of those around him. He had given his all to the army, to Rachel, to his role as a father. But in the end, none of it had truly fulfilled him. He needed to find something deeper, something that wasn't tied to the fleeting circumstances of life. He needed to find peace, not in what he had lost, but in who he was.

He made up his mind. He would leave the army. He would leave behind the life that had defined him for so long. The war that had been waged inside him for years—between duty and desire, between obligation and love—was over. Mike needed to find a new path. A path that would lead him toward healing, not just physically, but emotionally and spiritually.

The decision was difficult, and the aftermath was even harder. Leaving the army meant giving up the one thing that had given him structure, discipline, and purpose for most of his life. But Mike knew that in order to heal, he needed to find something else—something that could give him the meaning he sought without the weight of the past hanging over him.

He enrolled in university with the intention of becoming a pastor. It wasn't an easy decision to make, and there were many moments when he doubted himself. The life of a pastor was nothing like the life he had known in the military. But it felt like the right choice. It was a calling that resonated deep within him, a way for him to rebuild not just his own life, but also the lives of others.

As he sat in his first theology class, Mike realized that he was beginning a new chapter—one that would require him to confront his deepest fears and insecurities. His brokenness, his pain, his grief—everything would be brought to light. But there was something inside him now, something that hadn't been there before: a sense of forgiveness.

Mike had begun to forgive Rachel. Not because she deserved forgiveness, but because he needed it. He couldn't carry the burden of resentment and hatred any longer. He understood that forgiveness wasn't about excusing the hurtful things people did. It was about releasing the chains that kept him tethered to the past. It was about choosing peace over pain.

And as he immersed himself in his studies, Mike began to understand the true meaning of love and faith. The more he learned about God, the more he realized that the essence of faith was not about the rules and rituals—it was about connection. It was about the love that transcended all barriers, the love that had been waiting for him all along.

The journey wasn't easy. There were moments when Mike wanted to give up. When the weight of his past threatened to crush him. But through his studies and through his growing understanding of God's love, he began to heal. He started to feel whole again, not because he had found someone else to replace Rachel, but because he had found something deeper within himself.

In his final year of university, Mike received a phone call that would change everything. It was Rachel.

"Mike, I know you probably hate me," she said, her voice shaky. "I—I don't know what to say. I've made so many mistakes. I'm so sorry for everything I did. I hurt you, and I don't expect you to forgive me. But I just... I wanted to tell you that I'm sorry. I know you're becoming a pastor now, and I thought maybe you could help me."

Mike was silent for a moment, his heart racing. He hadn't expected this. He hadn't expected her to reach out. But deep down, he knew what he had to do.

"I forgive you, Rachel," Mike said softly, his voice steady. "I've forgiven you for a long time now. I had to, not for you, but for me. I can't carry this pain anymore."

Tears filled his eyes as he spoke. Not tears of anger, but of release. He realized that he had already let go of the anger and resentment that had once held him hostage. He had forgiven her long before she had asked for it. And in that moment, Mike realized something important: forgiveness wasn't a one-time act. It was a process, a choice that he had to make every day. And it was the key to healing his own heart.

Over the years that followed, Mike embraced his role as a pastor, guiding others through their own struggles and helping them find peace in their lives. He married again, a woman who shared his love for God and for helping others. And though his journey had been filled with loss, pain, and betrayal, Mike knew that it had also led him to a deeper understanding of love and forgiveness.

Mike's story was one of redemption, not because he had been perfect, but because he had found peace in the midst of his imperfections. He had come to understand that life wasn't about avoiding pain or seeking approval—it was about embracing the love that was always available to him, even in the darkest of times.

And as he stood before his congregation, speaking the words of love and forgiveness that had healed his heart, Mike knew that he had finally found his true purpose. It wasn't to be a soldier, or a husband, or a father—it was to be a vessel of God's love, sharing that light with others who needed it most.

Mike had always believed that his purpose in life was to serve, to protect, and to live in accordance with the discipline he had been taught in the military. But as he grew in his understanding of God's love and his new role as a pastor, he began to see things in a different light. His eyes were opened to the truth that had always been there, waiting for him to discover.

Purpose, he realized, wasn't about what he did—it was about how he did it and the energy he brought to everything. It was about love.

He stood in front of his congregation on a Sunday morning, his voice steady as he spoke the words that had come to define his understanding of life. "The purpose of our lives," he began, "is to spread love.

It's as simple as that. Life is about how we interact with each other, how we treat one another, and how we choose to give and receive love. It's about being conscious of our decisions, of our thoughts, and realizing that we hold the power to shape our own reality."

As he spoke, Mike's mind traveled back to the time when he had felt so lost, so consumed by the pain of his past. Back when he had believed that his suffering was a reflection of who he was. Now, he saw clearly that suffering was not a part of his true being. It was not who he was at his core.

"You are not suffering," he continued, his voice filled with the conviction of his newfound truth. "You are a higher being, full of love and light. You are not defined by your mistakes or your pain. The real you—the one you've been searching for—is the one filled with love, with the energy of the universe, of God. When we remember how deeply we are loved by God, it changes everything. It changes how we interact with others, how we treat ourselves, and how we navigate the world."

Mike's words were not just teachings—they were a revelation, a message that came from the very core of his being. He had discovered that we are all capable of creating our own energy. We can choose to be energy creators or energy consumers. We can either contribute to the world with our love, or we can take from it, draining it and leaving others empty. The choice was ours.

"When we act from a place of love, we become creators of energy," Mike said, pacing slowly in front of the congregation. "When we make decisions based on love, we align ourselves with the highest form of energy. And when we learn to control our thoughts, we learn to control our reality. We can choose to focus on the positive, to focus on what we can give, rather than what we can take. This is the essence of life. This is what it means to be truly alive."

Mike paused for a moment, letting the words sink in. He could feel the weight of them, the truth that reverberated in his chest. This wasn't just a lesson—it was the truth that had set him free.

"Life is about interactions. It's about how we treat each other. It's about loving ourselves and others, even in the face of adversity. When we remember the love that God has for us, it changes how we approach every moment. It changes how we make decisions. It changes how we respond to the world around us."

Mike's mind drifted back to his time in the army, to the days when he had pushed himself to the limit, trying to meet the expectations of others, trying to prove himself worthy of love. Back then, he had been consumed by the idea that love was something to be earned. But now, he knew the truth—that love wasn't something to be earned. It was something to be given freely, without condition.

"You are not your circumstances," Mike continued, his eyes locking with those of his listeners. "You are not your pain. You are not the sum of your mistakes. You are a being of light, capable of infinite love. The world may try to tell you otherwise, but you must remember this: you are already whole. You are already loved."

The words felt powerful as they left his mouth, a truth that he had spent years coming to understand. He wasn't just talking about love in a romantic sense, or the kind of love we experience in relationships. He was talking about the kind of love that transcends all boundaries—the kind of love that exists in all things, in all people. The love that was present in every breath, every heartbeat.

Mike could feel it now—the love that had been with him all along. It wasn't something he had to seek out or earn. It was inside him, inside everyone. And when we recognize this love, when we remember who we truly are, it has the power to transform our lives.

"It's time we stop seeing ourselves as separate from each other," Mike said, his voice growing softer. "We are all connected. We are all a part of the same source, the same energy, the same love. And when we begin to see the world through this lens, everything changes. We no longer see others as obstacles, as threats, as enemies. We see them as a part of us. We see them as the same light, the same love, the same energy that flows through us."

Mike's heart swelled with gratitude as he spoke. He knew that this was the truth he had been searching for, the truth that had been revealed to him in his darkest moments. He was no longer the man who had lived for the approval of others, no longer the man who had tried to prove his worth. He was a man who had found peace in the love of God, in the love of himself, and in the love of others.

"We are not meant to suffer," Mike said, his voice filled with quiet assurance. "We are meant to give love. We are meant to be creators of energy, of light. When we remember this, when we remember who we truly are, we step into our power. We step into the fullness of who we are meant to be."

As he finished speaking, Mike took a deep breath and looked out over the congregation. He saw the faces before him—some filled with hope, others with doubt, and still others with confusion. But he knew that each of them was capable of embracing this truth, capable of recognizing the love within themselves.

In that moment, Mike felt a deep sense of peace. He had found his purpose. His mission in life was no longer about seeking approval or living up to expectations. It was about spreading love, about helping others recognize the light within themselves.

"Remember," Mike said, his voice calm but firm, "you are not your suffering. You are not your past. You are a being of love, and that love is all you need to heal, to grow, and to live your life to its fullest. When you live from a place of love, you become a beacon of light in the world."

And with that, Mike stepped back from the pulpit, a sense of fulfillment washing over him. He had found his calling—not as a soldier, not as a husband, not as a father, but as a vessel of love. And in that role, he knew that he would continue to spread the message of love and healing for the rest of his life.

10

A Glass Half Full: The Story of James

James had always been a people person. His quick wit and easy smile made him the perfect bartender at one of New York City's most popular restaurants. For years, he poured drinks and listened to the stories of strangers, offering advice or a comforting word when needed. The bustling nightlife and the constant hum of the city gave him purpose, and he felt alive in the chaos.

When COVID-19 hit, everything changed. The restaurant where James worked for nearly a decade went bankrupt. One day, he was crafting cocktails for regulars, and the next, he was standing outside the closed doors of the restaurant, the faint "For Lease" sign swinging in the wind. James felt adrift. His income was gone, and his connection to the vibrant energy of the city seemed severed.

Football became his only solace. Once a month, he'd attend local games, a ritual that connected him to simpler, happier times. The roar of the crowd and the smell of hot dogs reminded him of his youth when life was less complicated. But even those outings began to feel hollow as the weight of unemployment bore down on him.

After months of struggling to make ends meet in a city where the rent never paused, James made a drastic decision. He packed his bags and left New York behind, heading south to Florida. He found a small beachside apartment in a quiet town. The sound of waves crashing against the shore became his new backdrop, a soothing balm for his frazzled nerves.

In Florida, James decided he needed a change. He had grown tired of the late nights and unpredictable schedules that came with bartending. The pandemic had drained the joy out of it. Browsing through job postings one afternoon, he came across an opening for a paramedic driver. It wasn't glamorous, but it was steady, meaningful work—and that was what James craved.

Training as an ambulance driver was a whirlwind. James learned to navigate the sirens and flashing lights through crowded streets, balancing speed with precision. The job gave him a sense of purpose he hadn't felt in a long time. He was part of a team saving lives, and though he wasn't a paramedic himself, he felt pride in knowing that his role was critical.

But with purpose came a heavy burden.

James saw death almost every day—car accidents, heart attacks, overdoses. He witnessed moments of raw human pain and grief, faces contorted in anguish, and lives forever altered. He began having nightmares, vivid images of the people he couldn't save. The sound of sirens, once a symbol of urgency and hope, became a trigger for his anxiety.

His PTSD began creeping into his daily life. Simple pleasures, like walking on the beach or watching a football game, no longer brought him peace. He avoided social gatherings, afraid he'd break down in front of others. His mind replayed every emergency call, dissecting what went wrong and wondering if he could've done more.

After a particularly grueling shift, James decided he couldn't continue. He sat in his parked ambulance, staring at the steering wheel, his hands trembling. Tears streamed down his face as he realized the job was breaking him. He needed an escape, a new direction, or he would crumble under the weight of it all.

He handed in his resignation the following week.

With no clear plan in mind, James wandered through town. One day, he stumbled upon a small, family-owned wine shop with a "For Sale" sign in the window. Something about the shop drew him in—the warm, rustic décor, the rows of bottles glinting in the sunlight, the faint aroma of oak and fruit.

James wasn't a wine connoisseur, but he'd always appreciated the artistry behind it. He remembered the occasional wine-tasting events he had organized as a bartender. Those evenings had been some of the most enjoyable parts of his career—bringing people together, sharing stories, and discovering flavors.

Impulsively, James decided to buy the shop.

The first few months were a steep learning curve. James immersed himself in the world of wine, studying regions, grape varieties, and tasting notes. He connected with local vineyards and distributors, learning the stories behind each bottle. Slowly, the shop began to take shape, a reflection of his newfound passion.

He named the shop **"Coastal Vines"**, a nod to his beachside town and the vineyards that now defined his life. The shop became more than just a business—it was a sanctuary. James poured his heart into every detail, from the carefully curated selection to the intimate wine-tasting events he hosted.

People began to notice the warmth James brought to the shop. Customers lingered, sharing stories about their lives over a glass of Pinot Noir or Chardonnay. James found himself listening again, just as he had behind the bar, but this time, the setting was calmer, more personal.

One evening, during a wine-tasting event, a customer remarked, "You've created something special here. It's more than just a shop—it feels like a community."

James smiled, feeling a sense of fulfillment he hadn't known in years.

James's journey had been anything but smooth, but he began to see the beauty in it. Each twist and turn had brought him closer to understanding himself. He learned to let go of the past—the restaurant in New York, the ambulance sirens, and the pain of his darkest days.

Through his wine shop, James discovered a new purpose: to create moments of connection, joy, and warmth. He realized that life wasn't about avoiding pain but finding ways to heal and grow through it.

As the years went by, James's shop became a cornerstone of the community. Locals and tourists alike visited, drawn by the welcoming atmosphere and James's genuine kindness. He continued to attend local football games, this time with friends he had made in Florida. The roar of the crowd no longer felt hollow—it felt like home.

One day, as he sat on the beach watching the sunset, James reflected on his journey. He had lost so much, but he had gained something far greater: resilience, purpose, and a deep appreciation for life's simple pleasures.

The waves crashed against the shore, and James raised a glass of his favorite wine to the horizon. Life wasn't perfect, but it was his. And for the first time in years, that felt like enough.

One crisp evening, while sitting on the porch of his beachside home, James felt a sharp, searing pain in his chest. It was unlike anything he had ever experienced. The cigar fell from his hand as he clutched his heart, gasping for air. The world around him blurred, fading into darkness.

When James opened his eyes, he wasn't in his body anymore. He felt weightless, floating in an endless expanse of light. The sensation was unlike anything he had ever known—pure peace, warmth, and love radiated from every direction, surrounding him like a comforting blanket.

He noticed a figure approaching him, a man made of shimmering energy, glowing with a golden light. The man's presence felt familiar, yet otherworldly. James felt an overwhelming surge of love as the man spoke, though his lips didn't move.

"You are not alone, James. You never were."

The man touched James's hand, and suddenly, his entire life flashed before his eyes. It wasn't just memories; it was as though James was reliving them all at once. He saw the joy and pain he had brought to others—the smiles he'd shared, the kindness he'd offered, and the hurtful words he had spoken in anger. He felt everything from both perspectives: his own and the people he had affected.

It was humbling, and at times, overwhelming. James saw himself as a young boy, standing alone in the schoolyard after being teased. He saw himself serving drinks at the bar, listening to customers pour their hearts out. He saw the lives he couldn't save during his time driving ambulances. And he saw the pain he had caused others, often unintentionally.

"We are all connected," the glowing man said. "Every action, every word, every thought creates ripples in the fabric of existence."

James wept, not out of sadness, but out of understanding. He realized how deeply intertwined his life was with those around him, how even the smallest acts of kindness or cruelty could echo through others' lives.

As the life review ended, another figure appeared. This one was older, with kind, wise eyes that seemed to pierce straight into James's soul. The man smiled warmly and said, "You know me, James. I've been with you all along."

James tilted his head in confusion. "Who are you?"

"I am your intuition," the man replied. "I'm the voice that whispered to you when danger was near, the feeling that nudged you toward the right path. I've always been here, guiding you, though you didn't always listen."

Memories flooded James's mind—moments when he had felt an inexplicable urge to avoid a certain road or when he had hesitated just long enough to avoid an accident. He realized that this presence had been with him throughout his life, quietly steering him away from harm.

"I didn't always pay attention," James admitted.

The older man chuckled. "That's true, but you did more often than you realize. And now, you're here to learn the most important lesson of all."

The glowing man and the older man stepped aside, and James was guided to a new realm. It was vast and breathtaking, filled with angelic beings radiating pure love. James felt their energy envelop him, lifting him higher.

Before him, the universe unfolded in a way he had never imagined. He saw nebulas forming and dissolving, stars being born and fading away. The cosmos seemed alive, pulsating with energy and purpose. James understood, for the first time, the interconnectedness of all things—the stars, the planets, the people, the very atoms that made up his being.

"Everything is part of the same source," an angel said. "You are not separate from it. You are not just a body or a mind. You are a spark of the infinite."

James felt as though his heart might burst from the love and understanding pouring into him. He saw knowledge floating before him, shimmering like a living library. He realized that he could think of any question, and the answer would appear before him, clear and complete.

He tested it, imagining a question about why suffering exists. Instantly, he saw images and felt truths unraveling before him—how suffering often leads to growth, how it is an integral part of the human experience, and how love is the ultimate healer.

Just as James felt he had reached a state of ultimate peace, an angel approached him. Her presence was soft and gentle, yet firm. "James," she said, "it's time to return."

James recoiled. "No, I can't go back. This is where I belong. I've never felt such love, such completeness."

The angel smiled sadly. "Your journey on Earth isn't over. There are still lessons to learn, people to help, love to share. You are needed there."

James resisted, pleading to stay. But as the angel touched his forehead, he felt himself being pulled away from the light, back toward his body.

James woke up in a hospital bed, gasping for air. His chest ached, and he felt the weight of his physical body once again. Tears streamed down his face as he whispered, "I didn't want to come back."

But as the days passed, James began to understand. The experience had changed him profoundly. He no longer feared death, knowing it was not the end but a transition. More importantly, he realized the significance of his life on Earth—to spread love, create, and connect with others.

He quit smoking, determined to honor the body that carried his soul. He started sharing his story with others, opening their eyes to the beauty of existence and the interconnectedness of all things. His wine shop became a place of community and healing, where people could come not just for a bottle of wine but for a sense of connection and belonging.

James lived the rest of his life with purpose, knowing that love was the ultimate truth. And when his time on Earth finally came to an end, he embraced it with open arms, ready to return to the light he had once known so well.

11

The Lightning Strike

It was a humid summer evening, and the dark clouds that had been threatening all day finally opened up over the city. Alex Foster stood alone in the parking lot, twirling his car keys in his hand. He had just finished his shift at the office and was heading home, where his routine of takeout and a late-night TV marathon awaited.

The thunder growled like a restless beast, and a sudden flash of lightning illuminated the world for a fraction of a second. The air crackled with tension. As Alex pressed the unlock button on his key fob, a bolt of lightning shot down from the heavens with a ferocity he couldn't have anticipated.

It struck him directly. In that instant, Alex felt a surge of unbearable heat and light. Time seemed to stretch endlessly. He was no longer aware of his physical body but instead felt as though he were being pulled through a tunnel, one not bound by space or time. When he opened his eyes—or what he thought were his eyes—he found himself standing in a place he didn't recognize.

The world around Alex was surreal, a landscape painted with colors he couldn't name and lights that seemed alive. The sky shimmered with shifting hues, and the ground beneath him was a soft, glowing surface that pulsed gently, as if alive. The air was warm, but it carried a strange stillness, a silence that wasn't unsettling but rather serene.

He looked down at his hands—or what should have been his hands. They were transparent, faintly glowing with a pale blue light. He realized, with a shock, that he no longer felt the weight of his physical body. He wasn't breathing, yet he wasn't suffocating.

"Where am I?" Alex whispered, though his voice didn't sound the same. "You are between realms," a deep, melodic voice said behind him.

Alex spun around to see a figure standing there. The being was tall and radiant, exuding a golden light that didn't hurt his eyes but instead filled him with a sense of peace. Its features were indistinct, like a shimmering outline of a human form.

"Who… who are you?" Alex asked.

"I am a guide," the being replied. "And you, Alex Foster, have stepped beyond the veil of your world."

Alex blinked—or tried to. "Am I dead?"

The guide tilted its head slightly. "Your physical form no longer binds you, but you are not truly dead. You are here to learn, to understand."

"Learn what?"

The guide gestured around. "This is a realm of reflection and connection, a place where souls come to see the truth of their existence."

As the being spoke, the landscape around Alex shifted. Scenes from his life appeared in the air like floating screens. He saw himself as a child, playing soccer in the yard with his dad. He saw himself as a teenager, sitting alone in his room, drowning in self-doubt. He saw himself as an adult, going through the motions of work and life, feeling unfulfilled but never knowing why.

"It's all here," the guide said. "Every choice you made, every action you took. This is your life, reflected back at you."

Alex felt a pang of guilt as he saw moments he wasn't proud of: the arguments with his ex, the times he'd ignored his mother's calls, the coworkers he'd brushed off when they needed help.

Suddenly, the scenes shifted. Alex saw not only his actions but also the ripples they created. He saw his ex crying after their fights, his mother's quiet disappointment when he didn't visit, the loneliness of the coworker he had dismissed.

"We are all connected," the guide said, as if reading his thoughts. "Every action, every word, every thought creates ripples that touch others in ways you may never see."

Alex felt tears—or what he thought were tears—stream down his face. "I didn't know... I didn't mean to hurt anyone."

The guide's light softened. "That is why you are here. To understand. To grow."

The guide extended a hand—or a form resembling a hand—and Alex felt himself being lifted. The world around him melted away, replaced by a vast expanse of stars, galaxies, and cosmic wonders.

"This is the source," the guide said. "The beginning and end of all things."

Alex felt as though he were floating in the heart of creation itself. He saw stars being born and dying, galaxies spinning in intricate dances, and streams of light weaving through the cosmos like rivers of energy.

"Everything is connected," the guide continued. "Every star, every planet, every soul is part of the same tapestry. And you, Alex, are a thread in that tapestry."

Alex felt an overwhelming sense of awe. He realized that he wasn't just an individual living a small, insignificant life. He was part of something infinite, something beautiful.

The guide brought Alex back to the shimmering landscape. "You have seen the web of connection. Now, there is one more lesson to learn."

Before Alex could ask what, a figure appeared before him—his father.

Alex froze. His father had passed away years ago, and their relationship had been strained. They had argued often, and Alex had always felt like he wasn't good enough for his father's expectations.

"Dad?" Alex whispered.

His father's spirit smiled gently. "Alex, my boy."

Tears welled up again as Alex felt a flood of emotions—love, regret, anger, and longing. "I'm sorry," he said. "I'm sorry I wasn't what you wanted me to be."

His father stepped closer, radiating a warmth that Alex could feel even in his ethereal form. "You were always enough, Alex. It was me who couldn't see it."

The words hit Alex like a wave, washing away years of self-doubt and pain. He felt lighter, freer.

The guide appeared again, its golden light filling the space. "You have learned what you needed to, Alex. It is time to return."

Alex shook his head. "I don't want to go back. I've never felt such peace, such love."

The guide placed a glowing hand on Alex's shoulder. "Your journey is not yet complete. You have a purpose to fulfill."

Before Alex could protest further, he felt himself being pulled away, back through the tunnel of light.

Alex woke up on the asphalt of the parking lot, rain pouring down on his face. Paramedics were surrounding him, shouting orders, their faces filled with concern.

He gasped for air, his body aching but alive.

In the weeks that followed, Alex couldn't forget what he had experienced. The connection, the love, the lessons—it all stayed with him. He quit his job and began dedicating his life to helping others, volunteering at shelters, mentoring at-risk youth, and living with a newfound sense of purpose.

He never looked at the world the same way again, knowing that every action, no matter how small, could ripple across the universe in ways he might never see. And he vowed to make those ripples count.

As Alex lay on the cold asphalt, drenched in rain, he faintly heard the sound of a woman screaming. It was the cashier from the corner store. She was running toward him, her voice shrill with panic. "Are you okay? Oh my God, someone call for help!"

Her voice sounded distant, muffled, as though coming from underwater. Alex opened his eyes—or thought he did—and saw her face above him, pale and frantic. Yet, he couldn't feel his body. Everything seemed... disconnected.

He tried to move, to speak, but instead, he felt a strange pull. A realization washed over him, not with fear but with clarity: *I am not this body.*

For the first time, Alex truly understood. The physical body, his aches, his scars, his experiences—it was all temporary. The essence of who he was, his spirit, was infinite, eternal, a part of something far greater. The body was merely a shell, a costume that he wore for a short time in this world.

Alex felt warmth envelop him, a light so pure and radiant it defied description. It wasn't blinding, but it filled every corner of his awareness. He felt a surge of energy flow into him, a love so profound it brought tears to his soul—if such a thing were possible. It wasn't frightening. It was simply *the way it is.*

He was not alone in this infinite expanse. The presence he felt wasn't a voice, a face, or even a figure, but an energy—one that radiated peace, understanding, and unconditional love. It was God's energy, Alex realized. Not the stern, distant God he had imagined growing up in Sunday school, but a presence of infinite compassion and unity.

Alex let himself surrender to it, and in doing so, he felt something he never thought possible: a completeness that he had been searching for his entire life. Every doubt, every fear, every hurt seemed insignificant in the face of this overwhelming love.

As the energy surrounded him, Alex saw images start to form around him, as if the light itself was projecting them. He recognized these moments—they were pieces of his life.

There he was, a child, holding his mother's hand as they crossed the street. He saw himself scoring a goal at his middle school soccer game, the pride on his coach's face. Then came the darker memories: yelling at his ex during a fight, ignoring a homeless man who had asked for help, the times he had hurt others intentionally or not.

He didn't just see these moments—he *felt* them. He felt his own pain, his own joy, but also the emotions of those around him. He felt the sting of his harsh words through the ears of the person who had heard them. He felt the loneliness of the homeless man as though it were his own.

It was overwhelming, but it wasn't a punishment. The review was simply truth.

"Everything is connected," a voice seemed to whisper—not aloud, but within him. "Every action, every thought, every word. You are part of the whole, and the whole is part of you."

Alex began to understand. Life wasn't about achievements, possessions, or status. It was about connection. About love.

The review faded, and Alex was left floating in the warm, golden light. A wave of ecstasy swept over him, as though he were dissolving into the love that surrounded him. He felt no boundaries, no separation between himself and the infinite.

It was the most beautiful, profound experience of his existence. Nothing in his life—his happiest moments, his greatest successes—compared to this.

But then, a sharp pang shot through him, breaking the bliss.

He became aware of his body again, the cold asphalt beneath him, the rain soaking through his clothes. The cashier's voice was clearer now, filled with relief. "He's breathing! Oh, thank God!"

Alex groaned, pain radiating through his chest. He opened his eyes fully, his vision blurred but functional. The paramedics had arrived, their hands steady as they worked to stabilize him. He wanted to tell them what he had just experienced, but no words came.

Over the next few days in the hospital, Alex had plenty of time to reflect. The experience stayed with him, vivid and undeniable. He knew now what he had touched—the infinite, the divine, the truth of existence.

He longed to return to that place, to the love and peace he had felt there. As much as he loved his family and appreciated the life he had been given, nothing on Earth compared to that realm. But it wasn't his choice to make. He realized that he had been sent back for a reason. The love he had experienced wasn't just for him—it was for everyone. And it was his responsibility to share it, to embody it, to live it.

Alex's recovery was slow, but his spirit was strong. He began to see the world differently. Every person he met, every interaction he had, was an opportunity to share the love he had felt. He smiled more, forgave more easily, and gave more freely.

He started volunteering at shelters and soup kitchens, not out of a sense of obligation, but because he genuinely wanted to help. He reached out to old friends and repaired broken relationships.

Alex also began sharing his story—not just the dramatic part about being struck by lightning, but the deeper truths he had learned. He told people about the life review, the connections we all share, and the infinite love that binds us together.

Years later, Alex stood at a podium, speaking to a room full of people. He had been invited to share his story at a spiritual conference. As he spoke, he could see the impact his words had on the audience—the tears, the smiles, the nods of understanding.

"I used to think life was about what you could achieve," he said, his voice steady and calm. "But it's not. Life is about how you love, how you connect, and how you make others feel. We are all part of the same infinite light, and the more love we share, the brighter we shine together."

The audience erupted into applause, but Alex wasn't seeking validation. He was simply living his purpose, spreading the love and kindness he had been sent back to share.

And in his heart, he knew that when his time came again, he would return to that golden light—not as someone who had taken from life, but as someone who had given all he could.

As Alex shared his story with close friends and colleagues, he had hoped to inspire them or perhaps offer some insight into the deeper meaning of life. He spoke with passion about the golden light, the profound love he had felt, and the interconnectedness of all beings.

But instead of admiration, Alex noticed subtle changes in their behavior. His friends exchanged uncertain glances, their supportive smiles now tinged with hesitation. His colleagues at work grew distant, speaking to him less and avoiding eye contact during breaks.

"You okay, Alex?" one of them finally asked. The question wasn't about his physical health but something deeper, unspoken, as if they feared he was losing his grip on reality.

It stung. Alex realized they didn't see his experience as a profound spiritual awakening—they saw it as a sign that something was wrong. Maybe trauma from the lightning strike, maybe stress, or worse, mental instability.

After a while, Alex stopped talking about it altogether.

Silence became his refuge. He kept his experiences close to his heart, no longer seeking validation or understanding. But something within him stirred—a restless energy, a need to *move*.

One morning, just before dawn, Alex laced up his old running shoes. He hadn't run in years, not since his younger days when he used to sprint through fields and back alleys, feeling free and alive. Now, older and heavier, he didn't expect much. He just wanted to feel the rhythm of his feet on the earth again.

As he stepped out into the cool morning air, a faint golden glow illuminated the horizon. The world was quiet, peaceful, and still waking up. Alex took his first tentative steps, his legs sluggish at first but gradually finding a rhythm.

As he ran, something incredible happened.

The light of the rising sun seemed to wrap around him, warm and gentle, as though it were alive. Alex felt it—not just on his skin but in his soul. The same energy, the same love, the same presence he had felt during his near-death experience.

It didn't speak to him in words, but he felt its message: *I am here. I have always been here. Run, Alex. Feel alive.* For the first time in months, Alex smiled—a genuine, joyful smile.

Running became Alex's sanctuary. Every morning, he woke before dawn, laced up his shoes, and hit the quiet streets. The world in those early hours felt different, almost sacred. With each run, Alex felt closer to the divine presence he had encountered. The golden light of the morning became a symbol of God's love, a constant reminder that he wasn't alone. Even on cloudy days, when the sun was hidden, he felt that same energy, guiding him, taking care of him from a distance.

The act of running was transformative. It wasn't just about physical health—it was about connecting with something greater. The rhythm of his steps, the sound of his breathing, the cool air filling his lungs—it all felt like a form of prayer, a way to align his body, mind, and spirit.

As Alex's runs became a daily habit, he noticed subtle but profound changes in himself. The heaviness he had carried for so long began to lift. His thoughts became clearer, his heart lighter. He started to approach life with a newfound sense of gratitude and wonder. At work, his colleagues noticed the change. "You seem... different," one of them said cautiously. "I am," Alex replied simply, a soft smile on his face.

Though he no longer spoke about his experience openly, it was evident in everything he did. He treated everyone with kindness and patience, even those who had once dismissed him. He radiated a quiet joy that was impossible to ignore.

One morning, during a particularly long run along a quiet trail, Alex stopped to catch his breath. The sun was just beginning to rise, its golden rays piercing through the trees.

As he stood there, bathed in the light, he felt the presence again—stronger than ever before. It wasn't just around him; it was within him.

Tears welled up in his eyes as he whispered, "I know you're here. Thank you."

In that moment, Alex understood something profound: the divine wasn't just in the extraordinary moments—the near-death experiences, the visions, the overwhelming revelations. It was in the everyday, the small, quiet moments of life. It was in the sunrise, the rhythm of his feet, the breath in his lungs.

Alex continued his runs, not because he was chasing something but because he had found something. Each morning was a gift, an opportunity to feel alive and connected.

His smile became his constant companion—a reflection of the joy and peace he carried within. It wasn't a forced smile or a mask to hide pain. It was genuine, born from the knowledge that he was loved, that he was part of something infinite and beautiful.

And as he ran, with the golden light guiding his path, Alex felt certain of one thing: his purpose was not to convince others of his truth but to live it. To spread love and kindness in every interaction, to embrace the beauty of each day, and to carry that divine presence with him wherever he went.

Because he knew, deep in his soul, that the light would always be there, shining not just for him but for everyone willing to see it.

12

The Last Dream

Samantha Bennett was a vibrant 36-year-old woman, full of life and ambition. She lived alone in a cozy apartment in Portland, surrounded by plants that thrived under her care. Her days were filled with work as a graphic designer and evenings spent with close friends or curled up with her cat, Luna, and a good book.

One night, Samantha had a peculiar dream. In it, she stood in front of a large, foggy mirror. Her reflection looked back at her, but it wasn't quite her usual self. Her skin appeared pale, her eyes sunken, and her body frail. A voice echoed from somewhere unseen, soft but clear: *"Your body is unwell. You must take care."*

She woke up with a start, her heart racing. The dream lingered in her mind like an ominous shadow, the words echoing over and over. Samantha shook it off as a product of stress and went about her day.

The next morning, Samantha felt slightly off. There was a faint ache in her chest, and her energy seemed drained. Still, she dismissed it. "Probably just a cold coming on," she told herself, sipping her coffee. But by afternoon, the ache had grown sharper, and a wave of dizziness made her sit down abruptly.

Concerned, Samantha called her doctor and managed to get an appointment for the following day. "You're probably fine," the nurse assured her over the phone. "But it's good you're coming in."

That night, Samantha's unease deepened. Her chest felt heavier, and her hands trembled as she tried to eat dinner. Luna curled up beside her, sensing her distress. Samantha petted her absentmindedly, her thoughts racing back to the dream.

That night, Samantha dreamed again. This time, she was walking through a vast, empty forest. The trees were gray and lifeless, their branches reaching out like skeletal fingers. As she walked, she felt her body weaken with every step. Her legs grew heavy, her breath shallow.

In the distance, she saw a figure standing in the fog—a woman with a gentle, glowing presence. Samantha approached her, desperate for help.

The woman spoke softly: *"You must rest. It's time to let go."*

Samantha tried to ask what she meant, but her voice failed her. The woman touched her shoulder, and a wave of calm washed over her.

She woke up gasping, her body drenched in sweat. The ache in her chest was now unbearable. "Tomorrow," she whispered to herself. "The doctor will fix this."

Samantha spent the day at home, too weak to do much else. Her friends texted her, asking if she wanted to meet up, but she replied with a vague excuse. She didn't want to worry them. Luna stayed close, her warm little body a source of comfort.

By evening, Samantha was struggling to stay awake. Her breathing was shallow, her vision blurred. She tried to convince herself that she could make it through the night, that the doctor's appointment was just hours away.

But deep down, she knew. As she lay on the couch, the world around her began to fade. A strange peace settled over her, replacing the fear. She closed her eyes, and in that moment, the ache in her chest vanished.

Samantha found herself standing in a field bathed in golden light. The air was warm, the sky infinite. She felt weightless, free from the heaviness that had burdened her. In the distance, she saw the same glowing woman from her dream.

"You've come home," the woman said with a gentle smile.

Samantha looked down at herself. Her body was whole, vibrant, and strong. The pain, the fatigue, the fear—it was all gone.

"Was it meant to be this way?" she asked.

The woman nodded. "You knew, even if you didn't understand. Life is not about how long you stay, but how deeply you live. And you lived with love, kindness, and beauty. Your journey here is complete."

Samantha felt a wave of love and peace unlike anything she had ever known. She thought of Luna, her friends, and the life she had left behind. There was no sadness, only gratitude for the time she had been given.

When Samantha's friends found her the next day, peacefully lying on the couch, they were devastated. The doctor's appointment she had scheduled remained unfulfilled, a quiet reminder of how fragile life can be.

But those who knew Samantha well felt her presence in the days that followed—in the soft glow of the morning sun, in the gentle rustle of leaves, in the warmth of Luna curling up beside them.

Her story became a quiet inspiration among her friends, a reminder to cherish each moment, to listen to the whispers of intuition, and to find beauty even in life's fleeting nature.

Samantha was gone, but the love she had given remained, eternal and unending.

As she reflects on her life, the woman remembers the immense struggle she faced growing up. Being dyslexic in school was a quiet battle she fought every day. She tried to hide her struggles, avoiding attention by sitting in the back of the classroom, hoping not to be called on. The whispered laughs of classmates when she stumbled over words during reading exercises cut deep, leaving her feeling isolated and ashamed.

Determined not to let her challenges define her, she spent countless hours practicing reading alone at home. She would sit in her room with a flashlight, sounding out words over and over again until they became familiar. It wasn't easy—it was slow, frustrating, and exhausting—but eventually, her hard work paid off. By the time she reached her teenage years, she could read fluently, though she still carried the scars of those earlier humiliations.

Despite her victory over dyslexia, the thought of continuing her education after high school felt overwhelming. She decided not to go to college, choosing instead to carve a different path for herself. She found joy in simple things—gardening, cooking, and spending time with her family. These moments of peace felt like rewards for the storms she had weathered.

What gave her life its deepest meaning, though, was her connection with what she described as her guiding angel. From a young age, she had always felt a presence—a quiet, comforting force that seemed to steer her toward safety and purpose. When she was a child, it was the feeling that made her hesitate before crossing a busy street, saving her from danger. As an adult, it was the voice in her heart encouraging her to persevere when everything felt too hard.

She often thought about the dreams she had before her death. In her final days, she felt more connected to the divine than ever before. She understood that the angel she had felt throughout her life was there to guide her toward the ultimate experience of love and peace.

Looking back on her struggles with dyslexia, the laughter of classmates, and the moments of pain, she realized something profound: every challenge she faced had shaped her into the resilient, compassionate person she became. The lessons learned through difficulty weren't punishments—they were gifts. Her life had been a tapestry woven with pain and joy, struggle and triumph, each thread guided by an unseen hand.

In those final moments of reflection, she felt no regret for not pursuing higher education or achieving what others might call "success." Her fulfillment came from the understanding that her life had meaning—not because of grand achievements, but because of the love she gave and the lessons she learned.

When the time came, and she felt herself leaving her body, the angel she had always sensed appeared fully before her, radiating light and warmth. It extended its hand, not to lead her away from her life, but to welcome her into the next chapter of existence—a realm of infinite peace and love.

In that moment, she understood that life was never about perfection or achievements. It was about growth, connection, and the courage to keep going. As she moved into the light, she felt gratitude for every moment of her journey, knowing that it had all been exactly as it was meant to be.

As she drifted in the warm light, she felt an overwhelming sense of peace and clarity. The angelic beings surrounding her were vast and majestic, their presence radiating love and wisdom. Their energy felt familiar, like something she had always known but forgotten during her time on Earth. One of the angels, with a voice both gentle and commanding, spoke to her:

"You have the gift of free will, the freedom to be a spirit that chooses love. But your journey is not yet complete."

The words were comforting yet confusing. She couldn't understand why she had to leave such a perfect, harmonious place to return to the struggles of earthly existence. As the angel spoke, she felt another presence approaching—a presence that felt deeply personal, like coming home. It was her father.

He appeared before her, his essence shining with a warm, golden light. He looked just as she remembered, yet more vibrant, more alive. Tears welled in her eyes as she reached out to him, and he embraced her in a way that seemed to transcend touch. In that embrace, she felt years of longing, pain, and unspoken words dissolve into pure love.

"Dad," she whispered, her voice trembling with emotion.

"I've always been with you," he said softly. "Every time you felt alone, every time you thought of me, I was there. And I'll always be with you, no matter where you go."

She realized then that what the angel had said was true—our loved ones never truly leave us. Their presence is woven into the fabric of our lives, guiding and comforting us in ways we often don't recognize. She had felt her father's presence before in fleeting moments, in dreams, in the quiet stillness of her heart. But now, seeing him here, she understood that connection would never be broken.

"I want to stay here with you," she said, her voice breaking. "I don't want to go back."

Her father smiled gently. "I know. But you have more to do. More love to give. More lessons to learn. And when your time truly comes, we'll meet again, and it will feel like no time has passed at all."

The angels joined in, their voices resonating like a harmonious chorus. "The answer to why you must return is simple: love. Love is the purpose of life. It is why you were created, and it is what you are meant to create. Your journey is not over because your heart still has more love to share."

Tears streamed down her face as she pleaded, "But I don't want to leave. I feel whole here, complete. The world is full of pain, and I don't think I can face it again."

The angel who had first spoken to her knelt down, bringing its luminous form closer. "We only send souls back if they are meant to go back. And you, dear one, are meant to return. Trust that there is a reason, even if you don't understand it now. Your pain has a purpose. It molds you, strengthens you, and teaches you how to love more deeply."

She felt a gentle pull, as though something was tugging at the very essence of her being. The light around her began to dim, and the warmth of the heavenly realm started to fade. Her father kissed her forehead and whispered, "You'll always carry this love with you. Remember it when times are hard. I'm proud of you."

And then, with a rush of energy, she was back in her body.

The hospital room was cold and sterile, a stark contrast to the vibrant warmth of where she had just been. Pain coursed through her body, and she could hear the beeping of machines monitoring her vitals. She had been unconscious for two weeks, the doctors later told her. Her condition had been critical, and her survival was nothing short of a miracle.

In those first days back, the physical pain was almost unbearable. But the emotional pain of being torn away from the light and love she had experienced was even harder to endure. She cried often, not from sadness, but from the sheer weight of what she had experienced and the knowledge that she had to continue her earthly journey.

Gradually, though, she began to find purpose in her return. She shared her story with anyone who would listen, though she quickly realized that not everyone was ready to hear it. Some people looked at her with skepticism or pity, as though she had lost touch with reality. But others—those who had faced loss, pain, or moments of deep questioning—found hope and comfort in her words.

She spoke about the love that binds all of existence, the interconnectedness of souls, and the guidance that is always available if we open our hearts to it. She reassured people that their loved ones were never truly gone, that they could still feel their presence if they quieted their minds and listened with their hearts.

And every morning, as the sun rose, she would sit by her window, letting the light wash over her face. In those quiet moments, she felt the warmth of the angel's words and the love of her father, reminding her of the purpose that had been entrusted to her: to live with love, to give with love, and to be a beacon of light in a world that so often forgets its true nature.

As she continued to heal, both physically and emotionally, she became a quiet yet profound advocate for kindness, gratitude, and the power of positive thought. She realized that her near-death experience wasn't just a personal revelation—it was a calling to share the wisdom she had gained and inspire others to live with more love in their hearts.

She began to encourage small but meaningful acts of kindness in her community. Whether it was helping an elderly neighbor with groceries, volunteering at a shelter, or simply offering a smile to someone who seemed down, she found joy in uplifting others. Her message was simple but impactful: "Do good whenever and wherever you can. Even the smallest act of love can ripple outward and change the world."

Her days started with prayer, not just for herself but for the world. She prayed for love, peace, and understanding to fill the hearts of all people. When friends or neighbors confided in her about their struggles, she would suggest not only practical steps to improve their situations but also the importance of shifting their mindset.

"Start with gratitude," she would say. "Even when life feels heavy, there's always something to be thankful for. The fact that you're alive, breathing, and here is a gift. Appreciate the small things—like the sun rising, the ability to walk, the laughter of a child, or the beauty of a single flower. Gratitude opens the door to joy."

Her mornings became rituals of gratitude. She would sit on her porch, sipping tea as the sun rose, marveling at the golden light that painted the sky. In those moments, she felt closest to the divine presence she had encountered during her experience. The warmth of the light reminded her of the angels, her father, and the love that radiates through all creation.

She also spoke about the power of thoughts. "Your mind is like a garden," she would explain to anyone who listened. "Whatever seeds you plant will grow. If you plant seeds of doubt, anger, or fear, that's what you'll reap. But if you plant seeds of love, hope, and gratitude, you'll harvest joy and peace. It all starts with what you allow to take root in your mind."

For her, positive thinking wasn't about ignoring life's difficulties or pretending everything was perfect. It was about choosing to focus on what was good and beautiful, even in the midst of hardship. She knew how fleeting life could be and wanted to make every moment count by embracing it with a full heart.

Her message began to resonate beyond her small circle. She started a blog where she shared her experiences and insights, and her words began to reach people all over the world. She received messages from strangers who said her writings had given them hope during their darkest times. Others thanked her for reminding them of the beauty in their own lives, which they had overlooked in the chaos of daily living.

Despite her growing influence, she remained humble, always redirecting the praise to the divine love she had experienced. "I'm just a messenger," she would say. "The real credit belongs to the Source of all love. I'm only here to share what was given to me."

Her life became a testament to the power of love and service. She joined community efforts to help the less fortunate, organized fundraisers, and started meditation and gratitude workshops. She taught people how to slow down, appreciate the present moment, and connect with the divine in their own way.

But her favorite part of each day remained the simplest: her quiet time with the morning light. It was in those moments that she felt the most profound connection to the love she had experienced in the other realm. She would close her eyes, let the warmth of the sun wash over her, and silently thank the universe for another day.

Her life, though far from perfect, became a shining example of how love, gratitude, and positive energy can transform not only an individual but also the world around them. By focusing on the good, she inspired others to do the same, creating ripples of kindness that spread farther than she could have ever imagined.

And though she knew she would one day return to the realm she had glimpsed, she no longer feared death. She saw it as a return home—a reunion with the angels, her father, and the infinite love that awaited her. Until then, she was content to live her purpose on Earth: spreading love, cultivating peace, and showing others the beauty that exists in every moment.

13

Title: The Infinite Thought

John had always lived fast. His heart beat to the rhythm of acceleration, the roar of an engine beneath him, the wind slicing across his face as he zipped down open roads. A motorcycle was not just a means of transport to him; it was freedom, a reminder that life was fleeting and meant to be lived in the moment. He would often remind himself, "Life is a ride," as if the saying alone was enough to justify his choices.

That afternoon, the sun blazed hot above him, the kind of day that felt like a promise of adventure. John had just finished his shift at work and was looking forward to a ride through the countryside. The motorbike hummed beneath him, purring like a contented animal, as he swerved in and out of traffic with ease. He was careful, but there was always a sense of urgency, a part of him that wanted to push the limits just a little further. But on this particular day, the universe had other plans.

A car swerved into his lane unexpectedly, and without time to react, he collided head-on with it. The impact was brutal, his body thrown violently forward, the bike skidding across the road, leaving a trail of twisted metal and sparks in its wake. Everything went dark.

John's last conscious thought was a strange one: *"I didn't get to finish that thought."* And then, nothing.

When John regained his senses, he was no longer on the road, no longer in his body. The physical world had slipped away like sand through his fingers, and all that remained was... a vast, incomprehensible space. It was as if he were floating in nothingness, a black expanse stretching out infinitely in all directions. He couldn't see, touch, or feel anything—just a void.

His mind, now untethered from the limitations of his body, raced. He thought about his life, the places he'd been, the people he'd loved, and the dreams he'd left unfulfilled. But something strange happened. Thoughts that were once fragmented—those half-formed ideas, the things he never quite finished—now found their resolution in the quiet expanse.

It was as if the space itself could complete the incomplete.

The thought he'd had before the crash—the one about not finishing—was now suddenly whole. He understood everything he hadn't yet grasped. There was no confusion, no uncertainty, only understanding. He felt a sense of peace, not because he had answers, but because the very act of living and experiencing was now clear. It was like the universe had whispered to him that it wasn't about having every answer, but about embracing the ride, the process itself.

"Was this it?" John wondered silently, but the moment he questioned it, the answer filled him. *Yes, this was it.* But it was not an ending. It was a shift. A transition.

He thought of his family. His mother, who always worried about his speed, his reckless driving. His friends who had admired his courage, his ability to live without hesitation. The people he'd never said goodbye to. A twinge of regret flickered within him, but it was quickly replaced with a deep sense of love—an energy that filled the black space around him, a soft, all-encompassing warmth. His love for them had not vanished with his physical body. It was eternal.

And as if responding to his silent thoughts, a voice, not from anywhere but everywhere, spoke.

"You are not lost," it said, gentle and kind. "You are never alone. Love is eternal. And now, you understand. You are part of the whole."

The voice was comforting, and John had no need to question it. He felt no fear, no anxiety—just peace. He was connected to something far larger than himself, something that had always been with him, even when he hadn't realized it.

The space, once black and empty, began to pulse with faint light. At first, it was only a small glow, but it quickly expanded, filling the vastness around him. Shapes began to form, not with sharp edges, but with flowing, soft contours. The light seemed alive, responding to his thoughts.

John knew, in that moment, that everything he had ever wondered about life and death was true. Time wasn't linear here. There was no beginning or end. All was connected in one eternal now. The thoughts he had once dismissed, the questions he had been too busy to answer, the experiences he had overlooked—they all converged in this space, in this moment.

And then, in the distance, John saw a figure—faint at first, but then clearer as he focused. It was not a being with form, but a presence. It felt ancient and wise, and yet completely familiar. It was as though it had always been with him, guiding him. The figure radiated pure light, a light that did not blind, but calmed and soothed.

John reached out, not physically, but in thought, and the presence responded.

"I am not here to answer all your questions, John," the presence said, its voice like a vibration in his soul. "But I am here to remind you that all things, even your unfinished thoughts, have their time to come to completion. You are part of the cycle, part of the whole."

John felt a deep, profound truth in those words. There were no more questions. No more doubts. Everything had been, in some way, answered. It wasn't about what he had done or not done. It wasn't about reaching a destination. It was about being present in the experience of life itself. Every fragment, every unfinished thought, every moment was a part of the whole.

As the presence faded into the light, John's mind drifted toward one final realization—he had lived well. His life wasn't defined by the things he didn't accomplish, but by the love he had given, the joy he had experienced, and the lessons he had learned. There was no fear now. There was only a peaceful surrender to the inevitable, a peace that came from knowing that everything, even the hardest moments, had meaning.

The black space softened, and John felt himself drifting—his awareness expanding, embracing the infinity of existence. He realized then that life was not something that could be contained in a single body or a single lifetime. It was vast, boundless, and eternal. He had been part of it all along.

And with that understanding, the last thought that had once felt incomplete—the one before the crash—was now whole, resolved.

"I'm ready," John thought. And with that, he faded into the light, where everything was whole and complete.

As John continued to float in the light, a profound understanding began to unfold around him, as if he were absorbing it from the very essence of existence. The truth was simple, yet infinite: *We are more than just our bodies.*

The body, he realized, was a vessel—an instrument through which a greater consciousness could experience life in its many forms. But this body, as familiar as it had been to him, was only a temporary casing, a fleeting illusion. What was truly eternal, what was truly *him*, could not be confined by skin and bone, nor by time or space.

In the vastness of this place, John began to understand that every being, every particle, every moment, was part of an interconnected web of life. His spirit was not separate; it was part of everything.

His mind expanded beyond his own life, reaching outward, sensing the lives of others—each one, a thread in the infinite tapestry of existence. He could feel the lives of the people he had known, their joys and sorrows, their loves and losses, woven into the fabric of the universe, stretching out in every direction. He wasn't just John anymore; he was the sum of every experience he had ever known, and the sum of every experience of everyone he had ever encountered.

We are all part of each other, he realized, *woven together in this infinite web, where no being is truly alone.*

He saw the Earth, a small, fragile sphere in the vastness of space, teeming with life. It was as if he could see all of humanity in one expansive glance, each individual existing simultaneously in the grand dance of existence. He could feel their pains, their dreams, their desires, and he could feel the love they gave to one another, the moments of kindness that ripple through the world, like a stone dropped in water.

He saw his family again, his friends, and even the strangers he had passed on the street in his lifetime. He realized they, too, were part of him, just as he was part of them. It was as though all the boundaries between people—between individuals—disappeared. There were no separations. There were only connections, threads linking one being to another, stretching across time and space.

John felt a surge of emotion, a profound sense of gratitude for this understanding. It was as though every breath he had taken on Earth had been a prayer, a moment of connection with the infinite. Every small action, every gesture of kindness, was a stitch in the fabric of this great, boundless whole.

Then, he felt it—an overwhelming surge of love, a love that wasn't just for those he had known, but for everything. The trees, the oceans, the sky, the animals, the stars. It was as though the entire universe itself was pulsing with love, and he was one with it. This love was not limited by time or space; it was the force that bound everything together.

"Love," the presence in the light seemed to whisper, *"is the essence of all things. It is the force that unites, that creates, that holds everything together."*

John's awareness expanded even further. He saw the beginnings of stars, the birth of galaxies, the unfolding of time itself.

He understood that everything was born from the same source, and that same source was love. This love was not an emotion; it was the very fabric of existence. It was the force that breathed life into everything, that connected everything, that gave purpose and meaning to every moment.

"You are not separate," the voice said, as if answering the question he had not yet asked. *"You are part of the whole. All is one. And that oneness is love."*

John felt a peace unlike anything he had ever known on Earth. There was no fear here, no need for control, no judgment. There was only understanding and acceptance. He could feel the ebb and flow of life, the rhythm of existence, and it was beautiful beyond words.

As he floated in this boundless space, he understood that he was not gone. He was not lost. He was part of something much greater than himself, something that stretched beyond the stars and beyond time. He had always been a part of it, and would always be. The journey was eternal, and each moment of existence, no matter how brief, was a beautiful thread in the great weave of the universe.

And then, in a gentle, reassuring way, the light began to soften, and he felt himself slowly being drawn back. The space around him began to contract, and he felt his consciousness returning to his body, to his earthly form. But it was different now. He was no longer just John, the man who had lived on Earth. He was something more—something infinite, something connected to everything and everyone.

He felt the love of the universe still with him, guiding him, even as he returned to his physical body. And in that moment, he realized that he did not need to be in this vast space to feel connected to it. He carried it with him, always. The love, the understanding, the connection—these were not things that existed only beyond the veil of life. They were within him, always, waiting to be felt.

As John slowly returned to his earthly existence, he could hear the faint sounds of the world around him—life continuing on, as it always had. He could feel the ground beneath his feet, the air in his lungs, and yet he knew, without a doubt, that he was more than just a body. He was part of everything. And everything was part of him.

With that realization, John knew that he had a choice—to live fully, to live with love, and to share that love with the world. He understood that this was the purpose of life: to experience, to love, and to be connected to all things, for as long as the ride would last.

And with that understanding, he smiled. He knew that the journey was far from over.

14

The Coffee Shop by the Hill

Nestled in a tranquil village surrounded by rolling green hills, *The Morning Brew* was more than just a coffee shop. It was a gathering place for locals, a sanctuary for wanderers, and a second home for its owner, Emma. With her warm smile and gentle demeanor, Emma had turned the small shop into a beloved cornerstone of the community.

At 34, Emma had lived a life filled with ups and downs. She had come to this village to escape her past and find peace. Yet, she carried the weight of old wounds—decisions she wished she could undo, words spoken in anger, and the ache of unfulfilled dreams.

One of her most loyal customers was Mr. Albert, an elderly widower who visited the shop every day without fail. Albert was quiet and reserved, his frail hands often clasped around a cane, but his eyes held a deep kindness. Emma had grown fond of him, and over time, he had become like family.

One rainy afternoon, Albert came in holding a smartphone, his face twisted in confusion. "Miss Emma," he said hesitantly, "could you help me? My son set up this coffee app, but I can't make sense of it."

Emma chuckled softly, putting aside the tray she was carrying. "Of course, Mr. Albert. Let me show you."

They sat together at a corner table, and Emma patiently explained how to use the app. Albert's hands trembled as he tried to follow her instructions, but she guided him with the same patience she had learned to extend to herself.

"You're an angel, Emma," Albert said, his voice filled with gratitude. "I don't know what I'd do without you."

As time went on, Emma felt the pull of change. She had been running the coffee shop for nearly a decade, and while she loved her work, she yearned for something new—a challenge, a fresh start. After much thought, she decided to sell *The Morning Brew* and take a job in the city.

When she told Albert about her decision, his reaction broke her heart.

"Why, Emma?" he asked, his voice trembling. "This place isn't just a coffee shop. It's... it's you. What will I do without our mornings?"

Emma's own eyes filled with tears. "I'm sorry, Mr. Albert. I'll miss you too. But I need to see what else is out there for me."

Albert cried openly, and Emma hugged him tightly, promising to stay in touch. She left the shop with a heavy heart, unsure if she was making the right choice.

Emma's new job in the city was demanding, but she threw herself into it, determined to prove herself. However, within months, she began to feel unwell. Fatigue, unexplained weight loss, and persistent pain in her abdomen led her to see a doctor.

The diagnosis was devastating: stage two ovarian cancer. Emma felt her world crumble. She was alone in the city, facing a battle she wasn't sure she could win.

For weeks, she spiraled into despair. Her past regrets resurfaced, amplifying her pain. The memory of her abortion weighed heavily on her, filling her with guilt and sorrow. She had been young and scared at the time, believing it was the best choice. Now, unable to have children, she questioned that decision daily.

One cloudy Sunday, Emma wandered aimlessly through a park and found herself standing in front of a small stone church. Its doors were open, and the sound of soft hymns drifted out.

She hesitated. Religion had never been a part of her life. But something inside her—a quiet yearning—pushed her to step inside.

The church was simple yet beautiful, with sunlight streaming through stained glass windows. At the altar stood Pastor James, a man with kind eyes and a calming presence. He noticed Emma and approached her gently.

"Welcome," he said. "Is there something on your mind?"

Emma hesitated, then began to speak. She poured out her heart, confessing her fears about death, her guilt over the abortion, and the anger she harbored toward people who had hurt her in the past.

Pastor James listened intently, his face compassionate. When she finished, he said, "Emma, forgiveness is a powerful gift—not just for others, but for yourself. You must forgive those who have wronged you and seek forgiveness from those you have wronged. Only then can you truly find peace."

Emma nodded, tears streaming down her face. "How do I start?"

"Let's pray together," the pastor said.

They prayed, and Emma felt a deep sense of release, as though a heavy burden had been lifted from her shoulders. The pastor spoke of the inevitability of death, not as something to fear, but as a part of life's journey.

"Death is not the end," he said. "It's a transition. What matters is how we live and love while we're here."

In the weeks that followed, Emma began to change. She reached out to people from her past, apologizing for the ways she had hurt them. Some forgave her, while others did not, but each conversation brought her closer to peace.

She also forgave those who had caused her pain. She realized that holding onto anger only hurt herself. By letting go, she reclaimed her power and found a newfound sense of freedom.

Emma started to see beauty in the small things again: the warmth of the sun on her face, the laughter of children in the park, the chirping of birds. She no longer feared death. Instead, she embraced life with a renewed sense of purpose.

Her chemotherapy treatments were grueling, but she faced them with courage. Each session was a battle, but Emma refused to give up. She leaned on the strength she had found through faith and forgiveness, and slowly, she began to heal.

Months later, Emma returned to the village for a visit. She had completed her chemotherapy and was officially in remission. Her body was weaker, but her spirit was stronger than ever.

She visited *The Morning Brew* and found Albert sitting in his usual spot. His face lit up when he saw her.

"Emma!" he exclaimed, rising to embrace her. "You look... different. Stronger."

Emma smiled. "I've been through a lot, Mr. Albert. But I'm here. And I'm better."

They talked for hours, catching up on each other's lives. When Emma shared her journey, Albert's eyes filled with tears.

"You've always been strong," he said. "And now, you're even stronger."

Emma's journey had been one of pain, growth, and transformation. She had faced her fears, confronted her past, and emerged on the other side with a renewed sense of purpose.

She didn't know what the future held, but for the first time in a long time, she wasn't afraid. She was alive, and that was enough.

As she sat on a park bench, watching the sun set over the hills, Emma smiled. She had found peace—not in perfection, but in forgiveness, love, and the simple joy of being.

15

The Girl in the Shadows

The rain-soaked streets of the suburban town seemed perpetually gray, mirroring the life of sixteen-year-old Elara. She stood out in her high school, and not in a way that earned admiration. With her jet-black hair, heavily lined eyes, dark lipstick, and wardrobe filled with lace, corsets, and boots, Elara was the epitome of gothic elegance. Her love for vampire films, haunting novels, and melancholic music gave her a sense of identity, but it also made her a target.

In a school where conformity reigned supreme, Elara was an anomaly. The whispers followed her wherever she went.

"Look at her. Does she think she's Dracula's bride?"
"Is it Halloween already?"
"Freak."

Elara pretended not to hear. She held her books tighter, staring straight ahead, but each insult chipped away at her already fragile self-esteem.

Elara found solace in her bedroom. It was her sanctuary, with walls adorned with posters of her favorite gothic bands and movies—*The Lost Boys, Interview with the Vampire,* and *Dracula.* Candles lined her windowsill, their flickering light casting eerie shadows. She would curl up in her oversized armchair, lose herself in Anne Rice novels, or sketch haunting landscapes in her journal.

But the sanctuary couldn't shield her from the growing darkness within her. As the bullying intensified, Elara began to withdraw from her friends and family. The words of her classmates echoed in her mind long after the school day ended.

"Maybe they're right," she thought. "Maybe I am a freak."

Elara's descent into depression was gradual but relentless. She stopped eating lunch at school, not wanting to give her tormentors another reason to mock her. At first, it was a few skipped meals. Then it became days where she barely ate at all. She told herself she wasn't hungry, but deep down, she felt like she didn't deserve to nourish herself.

Her parents, though loving, were busy with work and didn't immediately notice the changes. When her mother commented that she looked pale, Elara shrugged it off as part of her "look." But inside, she felt hollow—both physically and emotionally.

Her reflection in the mirror became another tormentor. No matter how thin she got, she always saw flaws. She convinced herself that if she could just shrink enough, she might disappear entirely. The hunger pangs became her twisted form of control in a world where she felt powerless.

One morning, Elara fainted in the school hallway. Her classmates gasped, some out of concern, others out of morbid fascination. When the school nurse called her parents, the gravity of Elara's condition finally came to light.

At the hospital, doctors diagnosed her with anorexia nervosa. She had lost so much weight that her body was beginning to shut down. They explained that she would need to be fed through a tube to survive. The words felt surreal to Elara, like they were happening to someone else.

Lying in the sterile hospital bed, with tubes snaking from her nose to her stomach, Elara felt utterly defeated. The girl who once found beauty in darkness now felt consumed by it.

During her hospital stay, Elara was assigned a therapist named Dr. Collins, a woman with kind eyes and a gentle demeanor. At first, Elara was resistant, offering only monosyllabic answers and avoiding eye contact. But Dr. Collins was patient. She didn't push; she simply listened.

One day, after a long silence, Elara finally spoke.

"I just... I feel like I don't belong anywhere. Everyone hates me for being different."

Dr. Collins nodded. "It's hard to be different, especially when people don't understand you. But being unique isn't a flaw, Elara. It's a strength."

Elara scoffed. "Doesn't feel like it."

"It won't right now," Dr. Collins said. "But I promise, there's a world beyond high school. And there are people out there who will love you for exactly who you are."

Recovery was not linear. There were days when Elara felt determined to get better and others when she wanted to give up. But slowly, with therapy, nutrition counseling, and the support of her family, she began to heal.

She rediscovered her love for art, spending hours sketching and painting as a way to process her emotions. Her drawings became less dark and more introspective, reflecting her journey from despair to hope.

Elara also found an online community of goths and alternative individuals who embraced her quirks and celebrated her style. For the first time, she felt seen and understood.

When Elara returned to school, she was terrified. Would the bullying start again? Would she crumble under the weight of their words?

But something had changed in her during her recovery. She had learned to value herself, not through the eyes of others, but through her own. The insults still hurt, but they no longer defined her.

One day, a girl from her art class approached her at lunch. Her name was Lily, and she wore a vintage band tee and combat boots.

"I love your sketches," Lily said, smiling. "You're really talented."

Elara blinked, surprised. "Thanks," she mumbled.

From that moment, a friendship blossomed. Lily wasn't goth, but she was kind and open-minded.

She introduced Elara to a group of friends who shared her love for music and art. Slowly, Elara's world expanded.

Years later, Elara would look back on her teenage years with a mix of sadness and gratitude. The pain she endured had shaped her, but it hadn't broken her. She went on to study art therapy, determined to help others find healing through creativity.

She still loved vampire movies and dressed in black, but now she wore her style with pride. It was no longer a shield but a celebration of who she was.

Elara learned that beauty could be found in darkness, but it was the light she discovered within herself that truly saved her.

Years after high school, Elara had rebuilt her life. She had her struggles, but she also had her victories. Her art therapy practice thrived, and she found fulfillment in helping others find their light in the darkness. She had even begun to heal her relationship with herself, though the scars of her past still lingered.

One day, while browsing a local bookstore, she met Adrian. He was charming and unassuming, with a quiet intensity that drew her in. He noticed the book in her hands—an obscure gothic novel—and struck up a conversation.

"You have good taste," he said, smiling.

Elara smirked. "You have no idea."

Their connection was instant. Adrian wasn't like anyone Elara had met before—he was patient, attentive, and seemed genuinely fascinated by her world. For the first time in years, she allowed herself to be vulnerable, to believe that someone could love her for who she was.

Within two years, they were married in a small, intimate ceremony. Elara thought she had finally found her happily ever after. But happiness, she learned, could be as fleeting as the shadows she once clung to.

It started subtly—Adrian growing distant, spending more time with their mutual friends, especially Lily, Elara's closest confidante since her recovery. Elara dismissed her suspicions at first. "It's nothing," she told herself. "I'm just being paranoid."

But the truth was unavoidable. One night, Adrian confessed. "I've fallen in love with Lily," he said, his voice heavy with guilt. "I'm sorry, Elara."

Elara's world crumbled. The man she had trusted with her heart had betrayed her, and so had her best friend. It was a wound too deep to articulate, leaving her feeling utterly abandoned and unworthy of love.

For weeks, Elara moved through life in a fog. She couldn't eat, couldn't sleep, and couldn't escape the crushing weight of her despair. The echoes of her old insecurities returned with a vengeance.

One night, unable to bear the pain any longer, she made a decision. She gathered every pill she could find in her apartment, sat on her bed, and wrote a note:

To anyone who finds this,
I'm sorry. I just can't do this anymore.

With trembling hands, she swallowed the pills one by one. The world blurred around her as her body grew heavy, her mind sinking into a dark abyss.

When Elara opened her eyes, she wasn't in her bedroom. She was floating, weightless, in a vast expanse of white fog. She looked down and saw herself—her lifeless body sprawled on the bed, empty pill bottles scattered around her.

Her first instinct was panic, but then she felt it: a warmth enveloping her, a love so profound it brought her to tears. The fear began to fade, replaced by an overwhelming sense of peace.

A voice echoed through the void, soft yet resonant, speaking directly to her soul. *You are loved, Elara. You have always been loved, no matter what.*

She tried to respond, but no words came out. Instead, her thoughts seemed to flow effortlessly into the presence around her.

Who are you? she thought. *What is this?*

The voice replied with a gentle laugh. *Do not fear. There is no pain here, only love. This is one of many journeys you will take.*

Before Elara could process the words, images began to form around her, like a film projected onto the fog. She saw herself as a child, drawing pictures for her mother and making her laugh. She saw the kindness she had shown to others—the art student she had encouraged, the client she had helped through grief, the small moments of compassion that had rippled outward.

Each act of love and kindness filled her with warmth, a reminder of her worth.

But then the images shifted. She saw moments of selfishness, times when she had pushed others away or lashed out in anger. These moments stretched on, each one like an eternity, filling her with shame.

Why are you showing me this? she thought, tears streaming down her face.

Because every choice matters, the voice replied. *But do not dwell on guilt. Learn from it. Grow from it.*

The fog began to clear, revealing a luminous figure before her. It shimmered with a crystalline green light, its form humanoid yet other-worldly. There was an undeniable magnetism about it, a sense of wisdom and peace.

"Are you... God?" Elara asked hesitantly.

The figure laughed softly, a sound like wind through trees. "No, I am not God. My name is Aleksander. I am your guide in this realm."

Elara stared at him, a mix of awe and fear. "What happens now? Am I... dead?"

Aleksander's light seemed to pulse with reassurance. "You are not dead, Elara. It is not your time. You must return."

"But I don't want to go back!" she cried. "There's nothing for me there. No family, no friends. They'll be fine without me."

Aleksander extended a hand, the light radiating from him growing brighter. "You are wrong. There is still much for you to do. Lives to touch, lessons to learn. Your story is far from over."

Before Elara could protest further, she felt herself being pulled back. The warmth faded, replaced by a searing pain in her chest and a churning in her stomach. She woke in her bed, her body convulsing. Panicked, she stumbled to the bathroom and vomited violently for hours.

When it was over, she collapsed onto the cold tile floor, drenched in sweat and tears. She was alive. Despite everything, she had been given another chance.

The days that followed were grueling. Elara sought medical help and began therapy, determined to make sense of her experience. She didn't share everything about what she had seen—Aleksander, the voice, the review of her life—but she couldn't shake the feeling that it had all been real.

She threw herself into her art, pouring her pain and revelations onto canvas. Her work took on a new depth, reflecting both the darkness she had endured and the light she had glimpsed.

Slowly, she began to mend. She reached out to others, reconnecting with old friends and making new ones. She volunteered at a crisis hotline, using her story to help others find hope.

Years later, Elara stood in a gallery, surrounded by her artwork. Her newest piece, titled *Aleksander,* was the centerpiece—a luminous figure bathed in green light, its hand outstretched.

People came up to her, moved by the painting's message of hope and resilience. Elara smiled, her heart full.

She didn't have all the answers, but she knew this: she was meant to be here, to live, to love, and to create. And that was enough.

16

The Journey of Sam: From Homeless Boy to Millionai

Sam was only 15 when his world shattered. His parents, both alcoholics, fought constantly. Their anger filled the house, their shouting matches echoing through thin walls. When they divorced, it wasn't a clean break. His mother packed up and left without a word, and his father—a bitter, angry man—took out his frustration on Sam.

One evening, after an explosive argument over a spilled drink, Sam's father threw him out of the house.

"Get out! I can't deal with you anymore!"

Sam stood on the street, a small bag of his belongings slung over his shoulder. He waited for his father to calm down and let him back in, but the door stayed locked. Hours turned to days, and Sam realized he wasn't going back.

Life on the streets was harsh, especially for a teenager. Sam quickly learned that people weren't kind to someone like him. He sought shelter in stairwells, but residents would yell at him, calling him a vagrant, and force him out. Some called the police, who simply moved him along without offering help.

Sam understood why they treated him this way. At 15, he was already tall and broad-shouldered. His patchy beard made him look older than he was. Nobody saw a scared, hungry teenager—they saw a threat.

Desperation drove him to scavenge through trash bins for food. At first, he felt ashamed, but hunger quickly silenced his pride. He discovered that trash near malls and restaurants often held half-eaten pizzas, burgers, and sandwiches. It wasn't gourmet, but it kept him alive.

One day, while searching for food near a mall, Sam noticed a small flyer taped to a lamppost: *"Farmhand Wanted. Room and board provided. No experience necessary."*

Sam tore down the flyer, heart pounding. He'd been surviving on the streets for months, and the thought of regular meals and a place to sleep felt like a miracle. He didn't have a phone to call the number, so he walked to the address listed—a farm on the outskirts of town.

The farmer, a stout man named Mr. Whitaker, eyed Sam warily when he arrived. "You're young," he said, crossing his arms. "Can you handle hard work?"

"Yes, sir," Sam replied earnestly. "I'll do anything."

Life on the farm was tough but a blessing. Sam worked from sunrise to sunset, hauling hay, tending to animals, and repairing fences. In return, Mr. Whitaker provided meals, a small room to sleep in, and a chance to wash up. Though Sam didn't earn money, he was grateful for the stability.

Over time, Mr. Whitaker warmed to him. "You've got a good work ethic, kid," he said one evening, handing Sam an extra helping of stew. "That'll take you far."

But as Sam grew older, he realized he couldn't stay on the farm forever. He needed more than food and shelter—he needed independence.

At 18, Sam left the farm and moved to the city. He found a job as a salesman in a liquor store. It wasn't glamorous, but it paid enough for him to rent a small apartment. For the first time in years, Sam felt like he was building a life of his own.

Yet, he wanted more. He spent his evenings researching ways to earn extra money. One day, he remembered how much he had enjoyed working with his hands on the farm. An idea sparked: gardening.

Sam started small, offering gardening services in his free time. He printed flyers and handed them out door-to-door. His first few jobs were simple—mowing lawns, pulling weeds—but word spread quickly. Clients appreciated his dedication and hard work, and soon, he had more requests than he could handle.

By his late 20s, Sam faced a choice: keep juggling two jobs or take a leap of faith and focus solely on gardening. He chose the latter, pouring all his energy into building his business.

He registered his company, *Green Haven Landscaping,* and invested in better tools and a small truck. His business grew steadily, and by the time he turned 30, he had a team of employees and contracts with several commercial properties.

The next decade was a whirlwind of growth. Sam worked tirelessly, expanding his services and reinvesting his profits into the business. He took courses on landscape design and hired experts to elevate *Green Haven Landscaping* from a simple gardening service to a full-scale landscaping company.

At 40, Sam sat at a large oak table in his home, surrounded by friends, employees, and business partners, celebrating his birthday. The table was laden with food, laughter filling the room. He looked around, marveling at how far he'd come.

In that moment, it hit him: he was a millionaire. The boy who once scavenged for pizza in the trash had built a life beyond his wildest dreams.

That night, after everyone had left, Sam sat alone in his garden. The cool night air was fragrant with the scent of blooming flowers. He thought about the long, hard journey that had brought him here—the nights he'd spent sleeping in stairwells, the people who had turned him away, and the rare few who had shown him kindness.

He didn't feel bitterness toward those who had ignored his cries for help. Instead, he felt gratitude for the struggles that had shaped him.

With his success, Sam decided it was time to give back. He started a foundation to help homeless youth, providing them with shelter, education, and job opportunities. He visited shelters regularly, sharing his story to inspire others.

"You might feel like you're at rock bottom," he would tell them. "But rock bottom isn't the end. It's the foundation you can build on."

Sam's success didn't just bring him wealth; it gave him the freedom to explore the world beyond work. When he wasn't managing his landscaping company or mentoring young people, he sought solace in nature. Hiking became one of his favorite pastimes. He loved the sense of freedom it brought—the crisp air, the rustling leaves, and the satisfying ache of muscles after a long trek.

At 45, Sam felt like he had achieved balance. His body was strong, his mind was sharp, and his heart was full of gratitude. But life, as he knew well, was unpredictable.

One sunny afternoon, Sam set out on a trail he had been meaning to explore for months. The forest was alive with the sounds of chirping birds and rustling branches. He was halfway through the trail, pausing to take in the breathtaking view of a valley below, when a sudden, sharp pain shot through his stomach.

It wasn't like anything he'd felt before. It started as a dull ache, but within minutes, it became unbearable. Sam clutched his abdomen and sank onto the grass, struggling to catch his breath.

He thought it might pass, but hours ticked by, and the pain persisted. As the sun dipped lower in the sky, he realized he was stranded. Weak and disoriented, he managed to call for help.

At the hospital, tests revealed something Sam hadn't expected: a tumor in his stomach. "You'll need surgery," the doctor explained, his tone gentle but firm. "We caught it in time, but we need to act quickly." Sam listened, a numbness washing over him. After all he had endured in life, he thought he had left suffering behind. But now, faced with the fragility of his own body, he was reminded of how precious—and fleeting—life could be.

The day of the operation arrived. Sam lay on the hospital bed, staring at the sterile white ceiling. He felt a mixture of fear and acceptance. As the anesthesiologist placed a mask over his face, he whispered a quiet prayer, not knowing if anyone—or anything—was listening.

"Count backward from ten," the doctor instructed.

"Ten... nine... eight..."

Sam's consciousness drifted, but he didn't feel like he was sleeping. Instead, he found himself in a vast, dark tunnel. It wasn't oppressive or frightening—it felt inviting, almost comforting. Soft light glowed at the far end, and as he moved toward it, he noticed luminous orbs of energy passing by.

Each orb radiated a unique essence. Some were vibrant and fast-moving, others gentle and serene. Sam felt a deep connection to these orbs, as if they were beings—perhaps even people. He wondered if they were souls, each on their own journey.

In this place, there was no pain, no sorrow, no regret. Only peace. A profound sense of bliss enveloped him, a feeling more complete than anything he had ever experienced.

As he neared the light at the end of the tunnel, he heard a voice—not with his ears, but with his entire being.

It's not your time yet, Sam.

The words weren't a command, but a reassurance. He wasn't ready to go. He had more to do, more to experience.

When Sam opened his eyes, he was back in the hospital. The bright, artificial light was jarring, a stark contrast to the gentle glow of the tunnel. He felt groggy but alive. The surgeon smiled down at him.

"Everything went smoothly," she said. "You're going to be just fine."

Sam tried to sit up but winced at the soreness in his abdomen. Despite the discomfort, he felt a strange sense of clarity. He needed to tell someone about what he had seen.

When the doctor came to check on him later, Sam recounted his experience—the tunnel, the orbs of light, the overwhelming sense of peace.

The doctor listened patiently but eventually smiled. "It's not uncommon for patients under anesthesia to have vivid experiences," she said. "The brain can play tricks on us, especially under stress."

Sam nodded, but deep down, he knew what he had experienced wasn't just a hallucination. It was too real, too profound. It wasn't something he would ever forget.

The experience changed Sam in ways he hadn't anticipated. He began to see life through a new lens, valuing each moment more deeply. He wasn't afraid of death anymore—not because he welcomed it, but because he understood it was part of something far greater.

Sam continued to thrive, but he also made time for the things that truly mattered: spending time with loved ones, mentoring young people, and giving back to the community. He spoke openly about his experience when asked, not to convince others but to share the peace it had brought him.

As the years went by, Sam's gardening company flourished. But his proudest achievements weren't the business or the wealth—it was the lives he touched. Homeless youth who came through his foundation found hope and purpose. Communities thrived under his guidance and generosity.

On his 50th birthday, surrounded by friends, employees, and mentees, Sam raised a glass.

"To life," he said simply. "Every moment of it."

In the quiet moments afterward, Sam thought back to the tunnel and the orbs of light. He didn't know exactly what they were or what lay beyond, but he knew one thing for certain: life, in all its messiness and beauty, was worth every second.

And when his time did come—whenever that might be—he would be ready, not with fear, but with gratitude for the journey.

17

Peter's Journey: Finding Himself

Peter sat in his room, staring at the flickering candle on his birthday cupcake. The small flame danced, casting shadows on the walls as if mocking his confusion. He had just turned 18, the supposed threshold to adulthood, but he felt more lost than ever.

He blew out the candle, making a silent wish: *I just want to understand who I am.*

Peter always felt different. While the boys in his class talked about soccer, cars, and video games, Peter felt disconnected. He wasn't interested in roughhousing or competitive sports. Instead, he gravitated toward the girls in his class. They were easier to talk to, and their conversations felt genuine.

But his closeness to the girls didn't mean he felt romantic toward them. One of his classmates, Emma, had confessed her feelings to him a few months ago. She was kind, pretty, and smart—everything he should have wanted. But when she kissed him, he felt... nothing.

Peter spent hours questioning himself. Did he like girls? Did he like boys? Was he broken for not feeling the same way his friends did? His confusion grew, gnawing at his self-esteem. He didn't dare voice his thoughts aloud, fearing judgment.

He began spending more time alone, diving into online forums and reading articles about sexuality. The more he learned, the more he realized he wasn't alone. There were people like him—people who didn't fit neatly into society's expectations.

One evening, Peter decided to step out of his comfort zone. He had read about a gay nightclub in the city, a place where people were free to be themselves. His heart pounded as he approached the entrance, neon lights casting a rainbow glow on the sidewalk.

Inside, the music was loud, the lights were dim, and the energy was electric. For the first time, Peter felt like he wasn't pretending. He danced with strangers, laughed, and let himself be carried by the moment.

That night, he met Daniel, a 30-year-old man with a warm smile and an air of confidence. Daniel bought him a drink, and they talked for hours. Daniel made Peter feel seen in a way he hadn't before. He didn't judge Peter's confusion; instead, he encouraged him to explore and embrace his feelings.

Their connection quickly deepened. Daniel became Peter's first romantic partner, and while their relationship was exciting, it was also overwhelming. Peter couldn't ignore the age gap, nor the nagging feeling that he was diving headfirst into something he didn't fully understand.

Daniel introduced Peter to a world of new experiences—art, music, and philosophy. But he also introduced Peter to habits that weren't healthy. Drinking became a regular part of their

Months into their relationship, Daniel confessed something that shattered Peter's fragile sense of security: he was HIV-positive.

Peter's world spiraled. Though Daniel assured him they had taken precautions, Peter couldn't shake the fear. He immediately went to get tested. Waiting for the results was agonizing, and when they came back positive, Peter felt his heart break.

He was 18, barely an adult, and already facing a diagnosis that would change his life forever.

Peter's initial reaction was despair. He blamed himself for being naive, for trusting too easily. He blamed Daniel, too, though deep down he knew the responsibility was shared.

For weeks, he isolated himself, drowning in self-pity and fear. The vibrant boy who had once danced freely in the nightclub was now a shadow of himself.

It was during one of these dark nights that Peter stumbled upon an online support group for young people living with HIV. Tentatively, he joined a meeting. Hearing others share their stories—of pain, resilience, and hope—lit a spark within him.

He realized he wasn't alone. Others had faced the same challenges and found ways to thrive. Slowly, Peter began to rebuild his life.

Peter started treatment, adhering to a strict regimen to keep the virus under control. He educated himself about HIV, becoming an advocate for safe practices and awareness.

He also revisited the question that had haunted him for years: *Who am I?*

Through therapy and self-reflection, Peter came to understand that his sexuality wasn't a problem to be solved—it was a part of who he was. He didn't need to fit into a label or anyone else's expectations.

By the time Peter turned 20, he had come a long way. He was no longer the confused teenager searching for answers in all the wrong places. He was still navigating his identity, but he was doing so with confidence and self-compassion.

Peter began volunteering at an LGBTQ+ youth center, sharing his story to help others struggling with similar challenges. He also rekindled his love for art, finding solace in painting and photography.

Peter's journey wasn't easy, and he knew it wasn't over. But he had learned to face life's uncertainties with courage. He had discovered that even in the face of adversity, there was hope, love, and beauty to be found.

And as he stood in front of a classroom, sharing his story with a group of teens who looked at him with wide, curious eyes, Peter realized something: he wasn't just surviving—he was thriving.

For a long time, Peter carried anger like a heavy stone in his chest. He was angry at Daniel for not telling him about his illness sooner. He was angry at the world for making him feel different, for making him feel like he didn't belong. But most of all, he was angry at himself—angry for the choices he made, for the person he was, and for the life he thought he had lost.

Every night, as he lay in bed staring at the ceiling, the same questions haunted him: *Why me? Why did this happen to me? What did I do to deserve this?*

But time, as it often does, softened his anger. Through therapy, self-reflection, and countless conversations with people who cared for him, Peter began to see his life in a new light.

One day, while journaling—a habit he had picked up to sort through his emotions—he wrote something that surprised even himself: *What if everything I've been through happened for a reason?*

The thought lingered in his mind, growing stronger each day. He began to realize that his pain had taught him things he might never have learned otherwise. It had given him an extraordinary capacity for compassion, a deep understanding of suffering, and a desire to help others heal.

Forgiveness didn't come easily, but it came. Peter reached a point where he could think of Daniel without bitterness. He understood that Daniel had his own struggles and mistakes. He forgave Daniel not because he excused what had happened, but because he didn't want to carry the weight of resentment anymore.

More importantly, Peter forgave himself. He forgave himself for being different, for the mistakes he made, and for the years he spent trying to fit into a mold that was never meant for him. He looked in the mirror one day, really looked, and said aloud: *I'm okay just as I am. I'm worthy of love, of happiness, and of life.*

Peter's health stabilized thanks to early treatment, and his doctor reassured him that with proper care, he could live a long and fulfilling life. That knowledge lifted a heavy burden off his shoulders. He was determined not to waste the gift of time.

He reconnected with friends and family who had stood by him during his darkest days. He spent weekends laughing over dinner with his sister, walking in the park with his childhood friend, and playing board games with his nieces and nephews.

Peter also dedicated himself to volunteering, working with organizations that supported people living with HIV and young LGBTQ+ individuals. He shared his story with anyone who needed to hear it, not to gain sympathy, but to show them that life could go on—that life could still be beautiful.

Peter's outlook on life transformed. He began to see every sunrise as a gift, every hug as a treasure, and every moment with loved ones as sacred.

One night, as he drifted off to sleep, he had a dream. In the dream, he was standing in a serene meadow bathed in golden light. A figure appeared before him—gentle, radiant, and filled with an indescribable warmth. It was Jesus.

Peter felt no fear, no shame, only an overwhelming sense of love. He looked into Jesus' eyes and saw acceptance, compassion, and understanding. Jesus smiled at him, as if to say, *I know you. I see you. And I love you just as you are.*

Peter woke up with tears streaming down his face. For the first time in years, he felt a deep peace settle over him. He whispered to himself, "That was a sign. Everything is going to be alright."

From that day on, Peter lived with a renewed sense of purpose. He didn't take a single moment for granted. He poured his love into the people around him, into the causes he believed in, and into himself. He continued to grow, to learn, and to heal.

Peter knew life would still have its challenges. But he also knew he wasn't alone—he had friends, family, and the quiet assurance of a love greater than he could comprehend.

And as he sat in his favorite café one sunny afternoon, writing in his journal, he smiled. For the first time in a long time, Peter wasn't just surviving. He was truly living, filled with hope, love, and gratitude for the journey that had brought him here.

18

Elisabeth's Journey: Strength, Friendship, and Sel

Elisabeth was no stranger to being the target of jokes. As far back as she could remember, her weight had been a source of mockery. In school, her classmates whispered behind her back, scribbled cruel nicknames on her desk, and sometimes even made mooing noises when she walked by.

But Elisabeth wasn't the type to shrink into herself. One day, when a group of boys cornered her during recess, laughing at her as she clutched her lunchbox, she decided enough was enough. Without hesitation, she pushed the ringleader so hard he fell into the dirt. "Say something else," she growled, her voice steady and fierce.

From that day on, nobody dared to tease her. Elisabeth wasn't just "the fat girl" anymore; she was the girl who didn't take nonsense from anyone.

Though her act of defiance earned her respect, Elisabeth knew there were others who couldn't fight back. One day, during art class, she noticed a smaller girl sitting alone at the back of the room. Her name was Mia, a quiet girl with glasses too big for her face and an ever-present sketchpad filled with anime characters.

The other kids called her names—"weird," "loser," and worse. Elisabeth saw the way Mia's shoulders hunched every time someone snickered at her drawings. Something about it stirred a protective instinct in her.

At lunch, Elisabeth plopped down beside Mia, much to the girl's surprise. "That's a cool drawing," Elisabeth said, pointing to a sketch of a warrior girl with flowing hair.

Mia's eyes lit up. "You like anime?"

Elisabeth hesitated but nodded. "Sure. Show me more."

From that day forward, the two were inseparable. They spent hours watching anime series, giggling over their favorite characters, and even trying to draw their own. For the first time, Elisabeth felt like she wasn't just defending someone—she was building a real friendship.

Elisabeth carried the confidence she developed in school into adulthood. After college, she landed a job at the local newspaper, starting as a junior writer. Her talent for storytelling and knack for sniffing out the truth quickly earned her promotions. By the time she was 30, Elisabeth was the editor-in-chief, running the paper with the same no-nonsense attitude that had once silenced her bullies.

Life felt good. She had a rewarding career, a cozy apartment, and even started dating. Her boyfriend, Mark, was kind, funny, and, as many women noticed, very handsome. Elisabeth wasn't oblivious to the way people stared when they saw them together. Women gave her jealous glances, and some even whispered behind her back: *What does he see in her?*

But Mark didn't care about the stares, and neither did Elisabeth. For the first time, she felt truly valued for who she was.

Life, however, had a way of throwing unexpected punches. Elisabeth's mother, her rock and biggest supporter, passed away suddenly. The loss hit Elisabeth harder than she expected. Her mother had always been her cheerleader, the one person who believed in her unconditionally.

Elisabeth fell into a deep depression. Every evening after work, she ordered a large ham and cheese pizza with a side of Coca-Cola. Cooking felt like too much effort, and eating became her only comfort.

Days turned into weeks, and weeks into months. Elisabeth's weight, which she had always carried with pride, began to feel like a burden. She avoided mirrors, hated the way her clothes fit, and felt sluggish all the time. Even Mark started to notice the change in her mood.

One night, as she sat on the couch surrounded by empty pizza boxes, Mark gently said, "Liz, I'm worried about you."

"I'm fine," she snapped, though her voice cracked. She wasn't fine. She was drowning in grief, using food as a lifeline that wasn't working anymore.

The real turning point came when Mia, now a successful artist and still Elisabeth's close friend, visited her unexpectedly. Mia didn't judge or lecture; she just listened. But before she left, she handed Elisabeth a drawing.

It was a portrait of Elisabeth as a warrior, just like the anime characters they used to draw together. Beneath it, Mia had written: *You've always been strong. Don't forget that.*

Something about the drawing shook Elisabeth. She realized that the girl who once stood up to bullies and took the world by storm wasn't gone—she was just buried under layers of grief and self-doubt.

Elisabeth decided to take small steps toward reclaiming her life. She started with therapy, where she worked through her grief and learned healthier ways to cope with her emotions. Cooking became a new hobby, and she found joy in experimenting with recipes that made her feel good physically and emotionally.

She also reconnected with Mark, sharing her struggles instead of shutting him out. His support reminded her why she loved him, and their relationship grew stronger for it.

Elisabeth even joined a fitness class—not to lose weight, but to feel energized and connected to her body again. The class was full of people of all shapes and sizes, and for the first time, Elisabeth felt no shame in moving her body.

Months turned into a year, and Elisabeth slowly found her way back to herself. She still enjoyed pizza nights, but they were occasional treats rather than nightly rituals. She worked hard at the newspaper, took time to draw with Mia, and went on long walks with Mark.

Most importantly, she learned to love herself again—not despite her size, but because of the person she had always been: strong, compassionate, and unyielding.

Elisabeth's story wasn't about becoming thin or perfect. It was about learning to face life's challenges with resilience and grace. And as she sat in her office one afternoon, editing the latest edition of the paper, she looked at the portrait Mia had drawn of her. It hung on the wall as a reminder of who she was and who she could be.

She smiled, knowing she still had so much to give—to her readers, to her friends and family, and most of all, to herself.

Elisabeth stared at her phone, the message from Mark still burning in her chest. It had been weeks since they had last talked, weeks since he had slowly faded from her life. He had become distant, his messages short and cold. When she reached out to him, desperate for clarity, the words he spoke shattered her. He had told her that they needed to talk, but the conversation that followed was one she had never anticipated.

"I think it's over between us," Mark had said softly, the words cutting through her heart like a cold knife.

"But... why?" Elisabeth's voice trembled, the question coming out more as a plea than anything else.

"I just don't feel the same way anymore," he replied, avoiding her gaze. "It's not you, it's me. I think we've drifted apart. I don't want to hurt you anymore."

The heartbreak was instant, sharp, and overwhelming. She had loved him. He had been her first love, her first real relationship. She had imagined a future together, maybe marriage, a family, a life. But now all of that was gone.

The grief and loss from her mother's death had already weighed heavily on Elisabeth's heart. Losing Mark felt like the final blow, like the universe was taking away the few things that had ever brought her happiness. She sank into despair.

To cope with the unbearable pain, Elisabeth turned to food. It was the one thing that offered comfort, however temporary. She found solace in indulging in ice cream late at night, sinking into the sweetness and the cold, drowning her sorrows in sugar. Sandwiches piled high with mayonnaise, cheese, and white bread became her go-to meal. The food didn't judge her, didn't make her feel small or unworthy.

She ate until she could eat no more, and then, after the fleeting sense of comfort faded, she ate again. As the days turned into weeks, Elisabeth's body changed. She grew heavier, her clothes tighter, and her energy drained. She felt sluggish all the time, constantly tired. Even simple tasks like going to the grocery store or walking to her car felt like monumental challenges.

Her thighs rubbed together when she walked, causing painful friction, and she found herself out of breath just from moving around the house. The depression worsened, and she often stayed in bed, binge-watching TV shows to distract herself from the void inside her. The thought of leaving her apartment, of facing the world outside, seemed impossible. She wanted to stay cocooned, hidden from the world, where the pain couldn't reach her.

One day, when she went to see her doctor for a routine check-up, the news hit hard. After running some tests, the doctor told her that she had developed diabetes. The words felt like another weight dropped onto her already burdened soul.

"Your blood sugar levels are extremely high," the doctor explained. "If you don't start making some changes, you could face serious health complications in the future."

Elisabeth nodded, but inside, she felt defeated. How had she let it get this far? She knew that her lifestyle—the overeating, the neglecting of her health—had led her down this path. She had been using food as a crutch to numb the pain, but it was now costing her more than she had ever imagined.

It was shortly after her diagnosis that something strange happened. One evening, as she lay on her couch feeling more miserable than ever, she felt an intense pain in her chest. It came suddenly and fiercely, gripping her heart as though it were trying to tear it from her chest. Her breathing became shallow, and the world around her seemed to tilt. She gasped for air, but the pain only grew worse.

As her vision blurred, she felt herself slipping into unconsciousness. In the stillness, Elisabeth found herself drifting, floating upward. It was as though she had left her body behind. The pain faded, and in its place, she felt a profound peace, a sense of calm she had not experienced in a long time.

She opened her eyes—or, at least, it felt like she did—and found herself in a place of soft, warm light. It wasn't like anything she had seen before. It was beautiful, serene, and completely free of pain. The air felt light, and her body, for the first time in years, felt free from the burden of weight.

Then, a voice spoke to her. It wasn't from any one person, but it was a presence, a force of love and understanding.

"You have always been loved, Elisabeth," the voice said, calm and soothing. "Even when you couldn't see it, you were always surrounded by love."

Elisabeth felt tears well up in her eyes. "I miss my mother," she whispered. "She never got to be the mother I needed her to be."

The voice answered gently, "Your mother loved you in the best way she could. She gave you life when she was young and struggling. But you, Elisabeth, you are not bound by the past. You are free to choose your future."

Elisabeth closed her eyes, feeling the warmth of the love that surrounded her. She wanted to stay there forever, to bask in the comfort and peace, but the voice spoke again, this time with a tinge of sadness.

"It's not your time yet. You have more to live, more to give, more to learn. Go back."

With those words, Elisabeth woke up. Her body was still aching from the stress, but the sense of peace she had felt in that strange, warm place stayed with her. She felt something shift inside her—something clicked into place.

She got up from the floor, trembling slightly, but determined. She looked around her apartment, her messy, cluttered space. It was as though she was seeing it for the first time, with a new clarity.

"How could I do this to myself?" she whispered to no one in particular, tears streaming down her face. She hadn't realized how far she had fallen, how much of her life she had wasted in sadness, blaming herself for things beyond her control.

"I have to start loving myself," she said softly. "I can't keep doing this."

Elisabeth began to make changes, slow but steady. She started by adjusting her diet, focusing on healthier, more nourishing foods. It wasn't about losing weight—at least not at first—it was about taking care of her body, about honoring it in a way she never had before. She swapped out sugary snacks for fruit, added more vegetables to her meals, and learned to cook for herself again, experimenting with recipes that brought her joy.

The journey wasn't easy, and there were days when she wanted to fall back into old habits, days when the sadness seemed too much to bear. But Elisabeth remembered the voice, the love that had surrounded her, and it reminded her that she was worthy of a better life.

She also began to exercise, starting with small walks around the block. It was hard at first—her body was not used to moving in this way—but over time, she gained strength. She even took a job as a post office worker, sorting newspapers, and delivering them around her neighborhood. It gave her structure and routine, something she hadn't had for years. And it gave her the opportunity to be more active and move her body in ways that were healing, both physically and emotionally.

Months passed, and Elisabeth's transformation, though not always linear, was undeniable. She lost weight, yes, but more importantly, she gained confidence. Her diabetes was present, but she managed it with the guidance of her doctors. She had learned to move again, to run without pain, and most importantly, to smile.

Looking back, Elisabeth understood that the journey was never just about weight loss. It was about reclaiming her life, healing from the heartache, and finding peace within herself. She had been through so much, but she had emerged stronger, wiser, and more compassionate.

She no longer held onto the past or the pain. She no longer felt sorry for herself or blamed anyone for her struggles. Elisabeth knew that the love she had been searching for—whether from her mother, Mark, or anyone else—was already inside her.

19

"Roots and Revelations"

The bass reverberated through the walls of the house, an insistent rhythm that mirrored the beating pulse of the party. Sophia swayed to the music, her head tilted back, arms raised above her as if trying to catch the glow of the string lights overhead. She was the picture of carefree rebellion, her dark curls cascading down her back and her smoky eyeliner smudged just enough to suggest the night was still young.

A faint haze of marijuana clung to the room, mingling with the scent of spilled beer and expensive perfume. Sophia took a long drag from the blunt that had been passed her way, holding it for a moment before exhaling, the smoke curling around her like a veil.

"Hey, Soph, you good?" her friend Tara asked, nudging her with a plastic cup half-full of something neon.

"Perfect," Sophia replied with a grin that didn't quite reach her eyes.

In truth, she wasn't sure why she'd even come tonight. She loved the parties—the chaos, the music, the fleeting connections—but lately, a strange hollowness had started to creep in. Still, it was better than being at home.

Home was a battlefield.

Her mother, Elena, was a formidable woman with a no-nonsense demeanor and a relentless devotion to rules and discipline. Sophia's antics—her late nights, her drinking, her habitual weed use—were constant points of contention.

"Why do you insist on destroying yourself?" Elena had yelled just the night before, her voice trembling with a mix of anger and desperation.

"Destroying myself?" Sophia had shot back. "I'm living my life. Maybe you should try it sometime."

The argument had escalated, as it always did, until Sophia stormed out, slamming the door behind her.

Now, as she moved through the crowd, the memory of her mother's furrowed brow and tear-streaked face flickered in her mind. She shook it off, focusing instead on the thrum of the music and the fiery burn of vodka sliding down her throat.

Back at home, Elena paced the living room, the soft glow of a single lamp casting long shadows on the walls. She had tried everything she could think of to reach Sophia, but the chasm between them only seemed to widen with each passing day.

Elena had been young once, too. She remembered the allure of rebellion, the intoxicating freedom of stepping outside the lines. But she also remembered the cost—mistakes she had vowed her daughter would never have to make.

Yet here she was, watching Sophia slip further away.

"Where did I go wrong?" she murmured to herself, sinking into the couch.

The house felt empty without Sophia's laughter or even the sound of her music blasting from her room. It was a silence that Elena couldn't quite get used to.

The night wore on, and Sophia found herself sitting on the back porch, the noise of the party muffled behind her. The stars above seemed impossibly distant, a glittering reminder of a world far removed from her own.

"You okay?" Tara asked, plopping down beside her.

"Yeah, just needed some air," Sophia replied, though her voice lacked conviction.

"You've been kinda off lately," Tara observed, her tone gentle but probing.

Sophia shrugged. "It's just my mom. She doesn't get it. She's always on my case about everything—what I wear, who I hang out with, what I do. It's like nothing I do is ever good enough for her."

"Parents," Tara said with a sympathetic laugh. "They're all the same."

But Sophia wasn't so sure. Deep down, she knew her mom's nagging came from a place of love, even if it felt suffocating.

For a moment, she considered going home, maybe even apologizing. But the thought made her stomach churn. It was easier to stay here, lost in the haze of the night, where the only thing that mattered was the next drink, the next laugh, the next distraction.

Sophia was leaning against the kitchen counter when a boy walked up to her at the party. His name was Ryan—at least, she thought it was. He had tousled hair, a charming grin, and a swagger that suggested he owned the room.

"You look like you're having a terrible time," he teased, handing her a drink.

Sophia smirked, swirling the liquid in her cup. "I could say the same about you."

They exchanged banter, the kind that felt easy and electric, fueled by alcohol and the buzz of the party. Before she knew it, they were out on the porch, sitting close. His arm brushed hers, and the next moment, their lips met.

It wasn't love, or even infatuation—it was escapism. The kiss was sloppy and fleeting, a blur in the haze of the night.

The next morning, a pounding knock jolted Sophia awake. Her head throbbed, and her mouth was dry as sandpaper.

"Coming!" she groaned, stumbling out of bed and toward the door.

When she opened it, a girl she didn't recognize stood there, her face twisted with anger.

"Who the hell are you?" Sophia asked, squinting in the harsh daylight.

The girl didn't answer. Instead, she lunged forward, landing a slap that stung Sophia's cheek and sent her stumbling back.

"You kissed my boyfriend last night!" the girl yelled, her voice shaking with rage.

Before Sophia could respond, the girl stormed off, leaving her standing there in stunned silence. She shut the door and leaned against it, her eyes welling up.

"What the hell is wrong with me?" she whispered, sinking to the floor.

The commotion had woken Elena. She marched down the hallway, her robe trailing behind her.

"What's going on now?" she demanded, her voice sharp.

Sophia looked up, her face flushed with shame and anger. "Nothing. Just leave me alone."

"Leave you alone? How can I when you bring this nonsense into our home?" Elena snapped.

Sophia jumped to her feet, her fists clenched. "Why can't you just let me live my life? You're always so controlling! You never let me do anything!"

Elena's face softened for a moment, but her voice remained firm. "I'm trying to protect you, Sophia. But you don't listen. You never listen."

Sophia stormed out without another word, slamming the door behind her.

The air outside was crisp, a sharp contrast to the suffocating tension at home. Sophia wandered aimlessly until she spotted the girl from earlier at a bus stop down the street.

Her anger bubbled over. She marched toward the girl, her fists clenched.

"Hey, you stupid!" she yelled. "Who the hell gave you the right to come to my house?"

The girl turned, her expression calm but cold. "You kissed my boyfriend. That's all the reason I need."

Before Sophia could reply, a car pulled up to the bus stop. The doors opened, and four girls climbed out, each of them glaring at her.

Sophia's heart sank, but she stood her ground. "What is this, a gang?" she scoffed, trying to mask her fear.

They didn't answer. The first punch landed squarely on her jaw, followed by another to her stomach. She tried to fight back, but the odds were against her.

The world blurred as she fell to the ground. Her head struck the pavement, and the sounds around her became muffled.

As her vision dimmed, she felt her body lift, weightless. She looked down and saw herself sprawled on the asphalt, blood pooling beneath her.

"This can't be real," she thought, panic creeping in.

An ambulance arrived, its sirens piercing the air. An older woman rushed to her side, shouting for help. Sophia wanted to cry out, to tell them she was still there, floating above it all, but no words came.

When she woke again, the world was a sterile white. The beeping of monitors echoed in her ears, and the faint scent of disinfectant filled her nose.

Her body ached, each breath a reminder of the beating she had taken. Tears streamed down her face as the weight of everything hit her—the fights with her mom, the chaos of her choices, the stark reality of her hospital bed.

Elena sat beside her, her eyes red and weary.

"Mom?" Sophia croaked, her voice barely audible.

Elena leaned forward, clutching her daughter's hand. "I'm here, sweetheart. I'm here."

For the first time in a long time, Sophia felt the sincerity in her mother's words. And for the first time, she wanted to listen.

20

"The Deep End"

The summer air was heavy with humidity, the kind that made clothes stick to skin and even the slightest breeze feel like a gift. Mark wiped the sweat from his forehead as he biked down the dirt path toward the river with his friends.

They were a rowdy group—Jake, the jokester who always had a sly grin and a half-baked plan; Logan, the quiet but dependable one; and Mia, whose fiery spirit could match Mark's own. They had spent countless summers by the water, but tonight felt different. The air buzzed with energy, the kind that made it impossible to sit still.

When they reached the bridge, Mark stopped and looked out over the river. The water shimmered in the fading light, inviting and serene. The bridge itself was old, with rusted railings and wooden planks that creaked underfoot.

"Anyone up for a jump?" Mark asked, his voice tinged with both excitement and challenge.

Jake raised an eyebrow. "From here? You're insane, dude."

Logan glanced down at the water, his expression doubtful. "We don't even know how deep it is."

Mia smirked, leaning on her bike. "Don't tell me you're chickening out already, Mark. Big words for someone who might back down."

Mark's pride flared. He wasn't about to let anyone think he was scared.

"Nah, I'm serious," he said, tossing his bike to the side and walking toward the edge of the bridge. "I'll prove it."

He climbed up onto the railing, balancing precariously as the others watched with a mix of awe and apprehension.

"Mark, maybe we should check first—" Logan began, but Mark waved him off.

"I've got this!" he shouted, spreading his arms wide like a bird preparing for flight.

The world seemed to slow as he took a deep breath, the adrenaline coursing through his veins. Then he leapt, the wind rushing past him in a blur of sensation.

The impact with the water was sharp and cold, shocking his system as he plunged into the depths. For a moment, he felt weightless, suspended in the dark, swirling world beneath the surface. But then something went wrong.

Mark opened his eyes, disoriented. The water was darker than he expected, the riverbed invisible below him. He kicked his legs, trying to surface, but a sharp pain shot through his left ankle. He realized too late that he had landed on something—a rock, perhaps—and his foot was caught in a crevice.

Panic set in as he struggled to free himself. The water pressed against him, and his lungs screamed for air. Above, he could see the dim light of the surface, tantalizingly close but impossibly far.

He yanked at his foot with all his strength, his heart pounding. His thoughts raced, images flashing through his mind: his mom laughing at the breakfast table, his little sister pestering him to play video games, the times he'd sat by this same river, carefree and invincible.

Above the water, the group realized something was wrong.

"Where is he?" Mia asked, her voice rising in alarm.

Jake and Logan ran to the edge of the bridge, peering into the water.

"He should've come up by now," Logan muttered, his usual calm replaced by a growing sense of dread.

Mia didn't wait for an answer. She threw off her sneakers and dove into the water, her instincts taking over.

The river was colder than she expected, and the current was stronger than it looked. She forced herself to focus, scanning the murky depths until she spotted Mark's figure below, struggling against something unseen.

Mark's vision began to blur, his body weakening with each second. Just as he felt the darkness closing in, a hand grasped his arm.

She yanked at him with a strength he didn't know she had, her determination cutting through his panic. With a final desperate pull, his foot came free, and they shot toward the surface together.

They broke through, gasping for air as the others shouted from the bridge. Logan and Jake ran down to meet them at the shore, helping to pull Mark out of the water.

He collapsed onto the grass, coughing and shaking, his ankle throbbing in pain.

"Are you crazy?" Mia yelled, her chest heaving as she glared at him. "You could've died, Mark!"

Mark looked up at her, his pride and bravado crumbling. "I didn't think..." he stammered, his voice barely above a whisper.

"No, you didn't," she snapped, but her anger quickly softened into relief.

Mark sat on the grass, shivering despite the warm summer air. His friends hovered around him, their relief palpable, but he wasn't paying much attention. His mind was elsewhere—still caught in the vivid, otherworldly experience he had just emerged from.

"You're lucky to be alive," Mia said, her voice quieter now but still tinged with anger.

Mark shook his head, staring off into the distance. "You don't get it, Mia. I wasn't just drowning. I was... somewhere else."

"What are you talking about?" Jake asked, exchanging a worried glance with Logan.

Mark struggled to find the words. "I was there, Mia. I was more than happy there."

"Where?" Mia pressed, crouching down in front of him.

"There. Wherever you go when you're not here." He rubbed his hands over his face, trying to steady his thoughts. "It was so bright, so full of light. The grass... it's greener than anything I've ever seen. And the air, it's like it's alive. It's so... peaceful."

The group fell silent, the weight of Mark's words settling over them like a fog.

"Are you saying you had a... near-death experience?" Logan asked cautiously.

Mark nodded. "I think so. When I was under the water, when I thought I wasn't going to make it, it just... happened. One moment I was panicking, and the next I wasn't in the river anymore. I was somewhere else."

Mia frowned. "Mark, you hit your head, and you were underwater for a while. Maybe you were just hallucinating."

"No," Mark said firmly, meeting her gaze. "It wasn't like that. It felt more real than this. More real than anything I've ever felt before."

Jake crossed his arms, his expression skeptical. "Okay, so what was it like? Did you see anything? Hear anything?"

Mark hesitated, trying to recall the details that were already beginning to fade, like a dream slipping through his fingers.

"I didn't see anyone, but I felt... something," he said slowly. "It wasn't a voice, not really, but it was like someone—or something—was there with me. Watching me. I felt... safe."

"Safe?" Mia repeated, her tone softening.

"Yeah," Mark said, nodding. "Like everything was going to be okay, no matter what. Like... I was part of something bigger."

The group sat in stunned silence, unsure of how to respond. Mia broke the quiet first.

"So, what? You think you saw heaven or something?"

"I don't know," Mark admitted. "But I know it wasn't just my imagination. It was... too real for that."

Logan looked thoughtful. "You've never really been into this kind of stuff before. You're not religious or anything."

Mark shrugged. "I know. But this wasn't about religion. It wasn't about anything I've ever thought about before. It just... was."

Jake tried to lighten the mood. "Maybe the river's water has some magical properties or something. You sure you didn't accidentally inhale a fish?"

Mia shot him a glare. "Not the time, Jake."

Mark managed a weak laugh, but his expression remained distant. "I know it sounds crazy. I don't expect you guys to believe me. But I know what I felt. And I know that... I didn't want to leave."

That night, after his friends walked him home, Mark lay in bed, staring at the ceiling. His ankle was wrapped, his body sore, but his mind wouldn't rest. The experience replayed in his head on an endless loop—the blinding light, the warmth, the inexplicable sense of belonging.

He wondered what it meant. Was it a glimpse of the afterlife? A hallucination brought on by oxygen deprivation? Or something else entirely?

The next morning, Mark couldn't shake the feeling that the experience had changed him. Everything around him seemed dull in comparison to the vivid beauty he had witnessed. The sky wasn't as blue, the grass wasn't as green, and even the laughter of his friends felt muted.

At lunch, Mia cornered him.

"Hey," she said, sitting across from him at the picnic table. "You've been quiet all day. Are you okay?"

Mark hesitated, then shook his head. "I don't know. I just... I feel like I shouldn't be here."

Mia frowned. "What do you mean?"

"I mean, I feel like I left something behind. Or like I wasn't supposed to come back."

"Mark, you're sixteen," Mia said firmly. "You've got your whole life ahead of you. Whatever you think you experienced, it doesn't mean you're not meant to be here."

He looked at her, his eyes searching hers for understanding. "What if it does? What if there's something I'm supposed to figure out now because of what happened?"

Mia sighed, running a hand through her hair. "Then figure it out. But don't shut the rest of us out while you're doing it. We care about you, Mark. I care about you."

Her words hung in the air between them, and for the first time since the incident, Mark felt a flicker of grounding.

As the weeks went by, Mark couldn't stop thinking about his experience. He started reading about near-death experiences, devouring stories of others who claimed to have seen the light, heard voices, or felt an overwhelming sense of peace.

He also began noticing small changes in himself—he was more patient, more reflective. The petty arguments and trivial pursuits that once seemed important now felt insignificant.

But the biggest change was in how he viewed the world. Every sunset, every breeze, every laugh with his friends felt like a gift. The mundane had become extraordinary.

One evening, as the sun dipped below the horizon, Mark stood on the bridge again, looking out over the water.

Mia joined him, her presence a comforting weight at his side.

"Do you think you'll ever figure out what it meant?" she asked.

"I don't know," Mark admitted. "But I think that's okay. Maybe it's not about finding answers. Maybe it's just about living differently because of it."

Mia smiled, nudging him playfully. "Well, let's start by agreeing not to jump off any more bridges."

Mark laughed, the sound carrying over the water. "Deal."

For the first time in a long time, he felt at peace—not just with what had happened, but with whatever lay ahead.

21

"The Weight of Years"

The old man sat in the corner of the small, bustling café, nursing a cup of tea that had long gone cold. His gnarled fingers toyed with the edge of his scarf as his eyes, still sharp despite his years, followed the movements of the world outside the window.

"You know," he began, his voice low and gravelly, "Lisa was one of the most remarkable women I ever knew."

His audience—a young journalist scribbling in a leather-bound notebook—looked up with interest. "Lisa?"

The old man nodded, his gaze distant. "She was a teacher. Dedicated her whole life to those kids. Spent forty years in the same little classroom, teaching everything from arithmetic to literature. She was the kind of woman who could make the unruliest child sit still with just one look. But it wasn't just about discipline; she had a way of making them believe in themselves."

"Did she retire?" the journalist asked, leaning forward.

"Oh, she retired, all right. But retirement wasn't easy for her. Lisa wasn't one for sitting still. The classroom was her stage, and when she left it, well... things changed."

Lisa sat in her dimly lit bedroom, her hands resting on the carved oak vanity she had owned since her twenties. She stared at her reflection in the oval mirror, the soft light highlighting every wrinkle, every crease, every mark that time had etched onto her face. Her once-rich auburn hair was now a cloud of silvery grey, and her eyes, though still sharp, carried the weight of decades.

She leaned in closer, tracing the lines around her mouth and the sagging skin beneath her chin. "This can't be me," she whispered, her voice trembling.

Lisa's mind drifted back to her youth. She could still remember the feel of summer sun on her skin, the way her hair gleamed like copper in the light, and the energy that coursed through her as if she could take on the world. She missed that girl—the one who smiled easily, danced without care, and didn't feel the weight of time pressing down on her.

Her thoughts took her further back, to a day she hadn't revisited in years. She was eight years old, running barefoot down the dirt road that led from the schoolhouse to her home. The sun was low, casting long shadows across the fields, and the air smelled of wildflowers and freshly cut hay.

She didn't see the car until it was too late.

The driver—a man whose breath reeked of whiskey—was speeding, his truck swerving dangerously as it barreled down the road. Lisa froze, her heart hammering in her chest. The impact came before she could move.

Everything went dark, and for a moment, Lisa felt nothing. Then, she was weightless, floating in a vast, endless void.

Out of the darkness, a light appeared. It wasn't harsh or blinding but warm and golden, like the first rays of dawn. As it grew brighter, Lisa saw a figure emerge—a being unlike anything she had ever imagined.

It was an angel, towering and radiant, its wings stretching out endlessly. Its face was kind, neither male nor female, and its eyes held a depth of understanding that made Lisa feel small and safe all at once.

The angel reached out, cradling her in its massive hands as if she were a fragile bird. Lisa felt a profound sense of peace, as though nothing in the world could ever harm her again.

"You are not meant to stay," the angel said, its voice like a melody that resonated in her very soul.

"Stay where?" Lisa asked, her voice tiny and uncertain.

"Here," the angel replied, gesturing to the light-filled expanse around them. "It is not your time."

"But it's so beautiful," Lisa whispered, tears filling her eyes.

The angel smiled gently. "One day, you will return. But for now, your journey is not over."

Before she could protest, the light began to fade, and Lisa felt herself falling. The peace was replaced by pain, sharp and overwhelming.

She woke to the sound of voices—her mother crying, the distant wail of a siren, and the drunken mutterings of the man who had hit her.

The memory was as vivid now as it had been then. Lisa ran her fingers over the scars on her leg, faint but still there, a reminder of the day she had danced on the edge of life and death.

She often wondered if the angel had been real or a figment of a child's frightened mind. But deep down, she believed. She had felt the angel's presence many times since then—in moments of despair, in the quiet of the night, and in the joy of seeing her students succeed.

The old man took a sip of his tea, his hand trembling slightly.

"She told me that story once," he said, his voice thick with emotion. "Said it was what kept her going all those years. Every time she felt lost or tired, she'd think of that angel and the promise of returning to the light someday."

The journalist looked up from his notes. "Did she ever talk about being afraid of growing old?"

The old man smiled faintly. "Oh, she didn't just talk about it—she hated it. Lisa loved life, but she hated what time did to her. Said she didn't like the stranger staring back at her in the mirror. But even then, she found a way to keep going. She always said, 'There's beauty in the journey, even if it's hard to see sometimes.'"

That night, as Lisa sat by her window, the moonlight casting a soft glow over her face, she whispered a quiet prayer.

"Thank you," she said, her voice barely audible. "For the time I've had, and for the promise of what's to come."

And for the first time in a long while, when Lisa looked in the mirror, she didn't see an old woman. She saw a life well-lived—a tapestry of moments, both beautiful and painful, that had shaped her into who she was.

The old man's voice softened as he leaned back in his chair, his gaze drifting to the café window. Rain began to tap gently against the glass, its rhythm matching the cadence of his words.

"She was my girlfriend once, back when I was in university," he said, almost as if he were speaking to himself. "Lisa and I... we were something special. Or at least, I thought we were."

The journalist looked up from his notebook, intrigued. "Lisa? The teacher?"

The old man nodded, a bittersweet smile playing on his lips. "Yes, Lisa the teacher. But before she was a teacher, she was just a girl with a fire in her heart and a dream in her eyes. And I was just a boy, hopelessly in love with her."

He paused, taking a deep breath. "We met in our second year. She was studying literature, and I was studying engineering. I used to see her sitting in the campus library, surrounded by a mountain of books. She had this way of tucking her hair behind her ear when she was concentrating—it drove me mad."

The journalist chuckled, sensing the warmth in his words.

"One day, I finally worked up the courage to talk to her," the old man continued. "I made some lame excuse about needing help with a poetry assignment. I was terrible at poetry, but I figured it was my best shot."

He shook his head, smiling at the memory. "She saw right through me, of course. But she laughed, and that laugh… it was like music. She said, 'You're terrible at lying, but I'll help you anyway.' And that was it. That was the beginning of us."

Their days together had been filled with laughter and light. They spent hours walking through the city, exploring bookstores and coffee shops, talking about everything and nothing. Lisa loved to read aloud to him, her voice bringing life to the words on the page. And he loved to watch her, the way her eyes sparkled when she spoke about the things she was passionate about.

"She wanted to be a writer," the old man said, his voice tinged with nostalgia. "She had this notebook where she'd scribble down ideas for stories—little bits of magic that only she could see. I used to tell her she'd be famous someday, but she'd just laugh and say, 'Teaching is my calling. Writing is my escape.'"

But as much as they loved each other, life had a way of pulling them apart.

"It was after graduation," he said, his tone turning somber. "I had a job offer in another city—a big opportunity that I couldn't turn down. Lisa wanted to stay and teach at a local school. Neither of us wanted to hold the other back, so we agreed to try long-distance. For a while, we made it work. Letters, phone calls, visits whenever we could manage. But it wasn't enough."

He sighed, his hands tightening around his cup. "One day, I got a letter from her. It wasn't long—just a few lines. She said she'd met someone else. Someone who was there, in her world, every day. She said she didn't mean for it to happen, but it had. And that was that."

The journalist watched him carefully. "How did you feel when you got that letter?"

"Devastated," the old man admitted. "Angry. Heartbroken. I couldn't understand how she could just... move on like that. I didn't realize then that it wasn't about not loving me anymore. It was about needing something I couldn't give her—a life we couldn't have together."

Years passed, and the old man built a life of his own. He married, had children, worked tirelessly in his field. But every now and then, his thoughts would drift back to Lisa. He wondered if she ever thought of him, if she was happy, if she still scribbled stories in that old notebook.

"I didn't see her again for decades," he said. "Not until a mutual friend passed away, and we both attended the funeral. By then, we were different people. She was older, greyer, but she still had that light in her eyes. The kind of light that made you believe the world was a better place because she was in it."

"And did you talk to her?" the journalist asked.

The old man nodded. "We did. It wasn't awkward, surprisingly. We talked about our lives, our families, the choices we'd made. She told me about her students, how much they meant to her. And she told me about her husband—the man she left me for. They'd been married for forty years. He'd passed away a few years before."

He fell silent for a moment, staring into his cup.

"It was strange, seeing her again after all that time. Part of me wanted to ask her if she ever regretted what happened between us. But I didn't. What would have been the point? The past is the past."

The journalist closed his notebook, sensing that the story was nearing its end. "Do you think you ever truly got over her?"

The old man chuckled softly, his eyes crinkling at the corners. "Oh, I moved on, if that's what you mean. But get over her? I don't think anyone ever truly gets over their first love. She was a part of my story, and I was a part of hers. That's enough for me."

He looked out the window, watching as the rain eased and the sun broke through the clouds. "Lisa taught me something, even after all these years. Life is messy and unpredictable, but it's also beautiful. And even when you lose something, you gain something else in its place. That's what she was to me—a lesson in love and loss and everything in between."

The journalist smiled, grateful for the glimpse into the old man's heart. "Thank you for sharing her story with me."

The old man nodded, a wistful smile playing on his lips. "She's worth remembering."

And with that, he turned back to his tea, content to let the memories wash over him like the gentle rhythm of the rain.

22

"Among Stars and Shadows"

Alina sat by the fountain in the heart of the lush garden that sprawled behind her family's estate. The scent of roses filled the air, but it was the sound of a pencil scratching against paper that held her attention. Across from her, on a small bench beneath an ancient oak tree, Adrian was sketching, his dark curls falling into his eyes as he concentrated.

"You've drawn me a hundred times," she teased, her voice light but full of affection. "Don't you ever get bored?"

"Never," Adrian replied without looking up. "Every time, I see something new. Like the way the sunlight catches your hair right now—it's golden, almost glowing. If I could capture that just once, I'd call myself a true artist."

Alina's cheeks flushed, and she laughed softly. "Flatterer."

But even as they joked, there was an undercurrent of tension that neither could ignore. Alina's family was one of the wealthiest in the city, their name synonymous with power and prestige. Adrian, on the other hand, was a scholarship student at a local art college, scraping by

181

on odd jobs and sheer determination. Their love was real, but it was also forbidden.

The day Alina's parents discovered the relationship had been nothing short of catastrophic. Her father, a stern and imposing man, had called Adrian "a penniless dreamer" and accused him of trying to take advantage of her. Her mother had been no kinder, suggesting that Alina's infatuation would fade as soon as she found someone "more suitable."

But Alina had stood her ground. "I love him," she'd said, her voice trembling but resolute. "And nothing you say will change that."

Her father's face had darkened with fury. "You don't know what love is," he'd snapped. "You're just a child playing games. When you grow up, you'll see how foolish you've been."

Alina had fled the house that night, her heart pounding as she ran to the small studio apartment Adrian shared with two other students. He'd held her as she cried, whispering promises that they'd find a way to be together, no matter what.

The months that followed were a whirlwind of stolen moments and secret plans. They talked of running away, of starting fresh in a city where no one knew them. But everything changed when Alina discovered she was pregnant.

Adrian had been stunned at first, but his shock quickly gave way to joy. "We'll make it work," he said, taking her hands in his. "It won't be easy, but we'll figure it out. I promise."

Telling her parents, however, was a different story. When Alina broke the news, her father's reaction was explosive. He accused Adrian of trapping her and threatened to cut her off entirely if she didn't end the relationship.

"You'll ruin your life!" he shouted. "Do you really think that boy can provide for you and a child? You're delusional, Alina."

"I don't care about money!" she fired back, her voice cracking. "I care about love. And Adrian loves me in a way you'll never understand."

Her father's response had been to banish Adrian from their home and tighten his control over Alina's life. But even that couldn't keep them apart. Adrian found ways to visit her, sneaking through the garden late at night or meeting her at secluded spots in the city.

As the pregnancy progressed, Alina's body grew heavier, and her emotions became a whirlwind. The strain of defying her family and planning for a future with Adrian was overwhelming, but his unwavering support kept her going.

One crisp winter evening, Alina sat by the fire in her family's library, her hands resting on her swollen belly. Her father entered, his expression unreadable.

"You're throwing everything away," he said quietly, his voice devoid of the usual anger.

"I'm choosing my happiness," Alina replied, her tone soft but firm.

"Is that what you call this?" He gestured to her stomach. "A child born into struggle and poverty?"

She met his gaze, tears welling in her eyes. "This child will be born into love. And that's more than enough."

The day of the birth arrived with little warning. Alina woke in the middle of the night to sharp contractions that took her breath away. The pain intensified quickly, and before she knew it, she was being rushed to the hospital.

Adrian arrived moments after her parents, his face pale but determined. He ignored the icy glares from Alina's father and took her hand, whispering words of encouragement as she labored through the contractions.

But something went wrong. The doctors' voices became urgent, and Alina felt the world spinning around her. The pain was unbearable, and then… nothing.

When Alina opened her eyes, she was no longer in the hospital. She was floating, weightless and free, in a vast expanse of space. Stars glittered all around her, and galaxies swirled like luminous ribbons. The silence was profound, yet she felt no fear—only awe.

A figure appeared before her, glowing with a soft, golden light. It wasn't human, but it wasn't entirely alien either. Its form was fluid, shifting like starlight, and its presence radiated a deep, comforting warmth.

"Where am I?" Alina asked, her voice echoing in the infinite void.

"You are between," the figure replied, its voice both gentle and powerful. "Between life and death, love and loss, hope and despair."

Alina felt tears streaming down her face, though she wasn't sure why. "Am I dying?"

"Your body is struggling," the figure said. "But your spirit is strong. You have a choice to make, Alina."

"A choice?" she whispered.

"To stay or to return," it said simply. "But know this: whichever path you choose will carry its own burdens and blessings."

Alina closed her eyes, her mind filled with images of Adrian, her unborn child, her parents, her life. She thought of the love she shared with Adrian, the life they dreamed of building together. She thought of the stars, how they seemed both impossibly distant and intimately close.

"I want to go back," she said finally, her voice steady. "I want to be with them."

The figure reached out, its light enveloping her. "Then go, Alina. And remember: even in the darkest moments, the stars are always there, waiting to guide you."

When Alina woke, she was in a hospital bed. Adrian was at her side, his face streaked with tears, and in his arms was a tiny bundle.

"You're okay," he said, his voice breaking. "You scared me so much, but you're okay."

She looked down at the baby—a perfect little girl with a tuft of dark hair—and felt her heart swell. Her parents stood at the back of the room, their faces etched with worry and something that looked like regret.

In that moment, Alina knew her life would never be the same. It wouldn't be easy, but it would be worth it. Because love, like the stars, was eternal—even in the face of struggle and sacrifice.

And so, she smiled, holding her family close, ready to face whatever came next.

The soft beeping of the hospital monitor brought Alina fully back to consciousness. Her body felt heavy, as if she were tethered to the bed, but her heart surged with relief when she saw Adrian sitting beside her, holding a tiny, wriggling bundle wrapped in a pink blanket.

"Alina, you're awake," Adrian whispered, his voice thick with emotion. He leaned closer, brushing a stray strand of hair from her face. "You scared me so much. But you're okay. We're okay."

Her parents stood a few feet away, their expressions uncharacteristically tender. Even her father, whose usual stoicism had been replaced by a worried furrow in his brow, seemed shaken.

"Alina," her mother said softly, stepping forward. "We thought there were complications... but the doctors assured us you're fine now. Please, look at your baby."

Adrian leaned down, gently placing the baby in Alina's arms. The world seemed to pause as she gazed at the tiny face before her. The baby's delicate features were framed by a shock of dark hair, and her little lips puckered as if she were already contemplating her first words.

Alina's breath caught in her throat. A warmth unlike anything she'd ever known radiated through her body, filling her chest with a love so intense it brought tears to her eyes.

"She's beautiful," Alina murmured, her voice trembling.

"She's perfect," Adrian said, his hand resting lightly on her shoulder.

The baby stirred, opening her eyes for the first time. They were a striking shade of blue, so clear and bright they reminded Alina of the stars she'd seen in her dreamlike journey through the cosmos.

"Hello, little one," Alina whispered, pressing a gentle kiss to the baby's forehead. "You're everything I ever wanted. Everything I never knew I needed."

Her father cleared his throat, drawing her attention. "Alina," he began hesitantly, his stern demeanor softened by the moment. "I... I misjudged everything. I thought I was protecting you, but I see now that I was wrong."

Alina blinked in surprise, her father's words catching her off guard.

"I've been stubborn," he admitted, his voice faltering. "I let my pride and my expectations blind me to what truly matters—your happiness. I see now that Adrian loves you. And you love him. That's what's important."

Tears welled in Alina's eyes as she looked at her father. For so long, she had yearned for his approval, his understanding. And now, at the most pivotal moment of her life, he was finally offering it.

"Thank you," she said softly, her voice breaking.

Her father nodded, his own eyes glistening. "You've given us a granddaughter. And I intend to be the kind of grandfather she can be proud of."

As the days passed, Alina recovered her strength, and the family began to find a new rhythm. Adrian moved into the guesthouse on her family's estate—a compromise that allowed them to remain close while maintaining some independence. Her parents, though still adjusting to the idea, grew to respect Adrian's devotion and his relentless determination to provide for Alina and their daughter.

They named the baby Stella, after the stars that had guided Alina back to life. The name felt fitting, a tribute to the ethereal experience she'd had during her near-death encounter.

"Every time I look at her, I'm reminded of how fragile and precious life is," Alina confided to Adrian one evening as they sat together in the nursery. Stella was asleep in her crib, her tiny chest rising and falling in a peaceful rhythm.

Adrian took her hand, intertwining their fingers. "She's a miracle," he said. "And so are you. I thought I lost you, Alina. When you were unconscious, I... I didn't know if I'd ever see you smile again."

Alina leaned her head against his shoulder, a tear slipping down her cheek. "I was somewhere else, Adrian. Somewhere beautiful. But I chose to come back because of you. Because of her. I knew I had to fight to stay."

Adrian kissed the top of her head, his heart full. "I'll spend the rest of my life making sure you know you made the right choice."

The months turned into years, and the young family thrived. Adrian's art gained recognition, his work capturing the raw beauty of love and resilience. His most acclaimed piece, *Stella Among the Stars,* was a luminous painting inspired by the night Alina gave birth—a night that forever changed their lives.

Alina, too, found her place. She became an advocate for young mothers, using her experience to support those who faced challenges similar to her own. Her strength and compassion inspired many, including her parents, who became vocal supporters of her efforts.

One summer evening, as the sun dipped below the horizon, Alina and Adrian sat on a blanket in the garden with Stella, now a spirited five-year-old. She ran barefoot through the grass, chasing fireflies and laughing with pure, unbridled joy.

"She's growing up so fast," Alina mused, watching their daughter with a mix of pride and wistfulness.

Adrian nodded, his arm around her shoulders. "She's incredible. Just like her mother."

Alina smiled, resting her head against his chest. "I never imagined life could be like this. Even with all the struggles, all the pain... it's worth it."

Adrian pressed a kiss to her temple, his heart full. "You're my everything, Alina. You and Stella. As long as I have you both, I have all the riches I'll ever need."

As the first stars appeared in the sky, Stella ran back to them, her arms full of glowing fireflies caught in a jar.

"Look, Mama! Look, Papa!" she exclaimed, her face radiant with excitement. "I caught the stars!"

Alina and Adrian laughed, pulling their daughter close. In that moment, beneath the endless expanse of the cosmos, they knew they had found their heaven on Earth.

Life, like the stars, was vast and unpredictable. But as long as they had each other, they could navigate any darkness, finding light in the love they shared.

23

The Smoke

Elena had always lived in the village of Korovets, nestled in a quiet valley where every face was familiar, every routine predictable. Life was simple, and though it occasionally bordered on monotonous, she found comfort in its steadiness. The same people shopped at the tiny market, the same greetings were exchanged on the cobbled streets, and the same church bell rang every Sunday morning.

Her apartment was modest, a single-bedroom unit on the second floor of a creaky, three-story building. It wasn't much, but it was hers, and after a long day at the textile factory, she looked forward to curling up on her faded brown couch with the television humming softly in the background.

It was just past 7 p.m. when she walked into her apartment, tossing her bag onto the chair by the door. Kicking off her shoes, she went to the kitchen, made a cup of tea, and carried it to the living room. The familiar tune of the local news theme played as she settled into her usual spot, the room dim except for the soft glow of the screen.

The first sign of something amiss came as a faint scent of burning. It tickled her nose, making her wrinkle it briefly. "Someone's overcooking dinner again," she muttered, a dry smile tugging at her lips. In the tightly packed apartment complex, it wasn't uncommon for kitchen mishaps to make their presence known. Once, Mrs. Boyko downstairs had burned an entire pot of borscht, and the smell lingered for days.

She dismissed it, focusing instead on the weather forecast. Snow was expected in a few days, and she made a mental note to dig out her heavier boots. But as the minutes passed, the smell grew stronger, sharper, and less like overcooked food. It was acrid now, biting, and it began to fill her nostrils, making her throat itch.

Elena glanced toward the window. The street outside seemed normal at first—dark, lit only by the occasional flicker of the lamppost. But then she noticed movement, faint figures emerging from the other apartments. Neighbors were trickling out, some carrying children, others holding jackets against the cold.

She squinted, confused, as she caught sight of a woman waving frantically in her direction. It was Mrs. Hrynenko from the first floor. The older woman's face was pale, and she was gesturing wildly, pointing upward and then toward the street. Elena furrowed her brow but stayed where she was.

"Probably just panicking," she thought. Mrs. Hrynenko was known for her dramatics. Once, she'd called the fire brigade because she thought a stray cat in a tree might fall and hurt itself. Elena shook her head, unwilling to let her evening peace be disturbed by what she assumed was another overreaction.

But then came a sound that made her heart skip—a muffled commotion in the hallway outside her door. She turned off the television and listened intently. Shuffling, hurried footsteps, and muffled voices. The smell was undeniable now, pungent and thick, making her eyes water.

Curiosity pushed her to her feet. She opened her door a crack and gasped. The hallway was filled with gray smoke, curling in lazy tendrils up the walls and across the ceiling. Panic gripped her chest as she realized this wasn't just another neighbor's burnt dinner—it was something far worse.

Elena coughed, slamming the door shut as smoke began to seep into her apartment. Her hands shook as she grabbed her coat from the chair, fumbling with the buttons. She needed to get out, but where had she put her phone? She spun around, searching the small room frantically. The coffee table? No. The kitchen counter? Not there either.

The smell was overpowering now, clawing at her throat. Her vision blurred as her eyes watered, and she could hear the distant wail of sirens. Someone must have called the fire department. Still, she couldn't leave without her phone—it was her only lifeline. Finally, she spotted it half-buried beneath a stack of old magazines on the table. She snatched it up, crammed it into her coat pocket, and slipped on her shoes.

By the time she stepped into the hallway, the smoke was so thick she could barely see the door to the stairs. Her lungs burned as she coughed violently, one hand gripping the railing as she descended. The world felt surreal, her familiar home transformed into a nightmarish maze of smoke and shadows.

Elena's heart pounded as she stumbled through the haze, her thoughts racing. What had caused this? An electrical fire? A forgotten candle? She had no answers, only the primal urge to escape. Each step felt heavier than the last, and she could barely make out the voices of others shouting below.

Finally, she burst through the main doors and into the freezing night air. She collapsed onto the pavement, coughing and gasping for breath. Around her, neighbors were clustered in small groups, some wrapped in blankets, others holding each other for warmth. The building loomed behind them, smoke billowing from the windows like a dark, sinister cloud.

The cold pavement pressed against Elena's cheek, a sharp contrast to the searing heat she had just escaped. She coughed violently, her lungs straining to expel the acrid smoke. Somewhere in the distance, she could hear voices—neighbors calling out, the wail of sirens cutting through the night.

Then, everything began to fade. The chill of the ground, the shouts, even the pain in her chest—it all ebbed away, replaced by a strange, weightless sensation. Her eyelids fluttered, and as they closed, the world around her dissolved into white.

When Elena opened her eyes, she was no longer outside her apartment. The whiteness stretched endlessly, neither blinding nor dim. It was soft, like light filtered through a cloud, and seemed to come from everywhere at once. She felt as if she were floating, though her feet rested firmly on a surface she couldn't see.

A strange calm washed over her. The coughing and pain were gone, replaced by an indescribable serenity. She turned her head, trying to make sense of where she was, but the expanse remained unbroken.

"Where am I?" she murmured, her voice echoing faintly.

"You are safe," a voice answered, soft yet powerful, as though it resonated directly within her mind. Elena turned sharply, searching for the source, but there was no one—just the endless white.

"Who's there?" she called out, her voice trembling. "What is this place?"

There was a pause, and then the voice came again, gentle and steady. "You are in a place between. A moment of pause before you choose your path."

"My path?" Elena frowned, her mind racing. The last thing she remembered was running out of the building, the smoke choking her lungs. Was she dead? "Am I... is this heaven?"

The voice didn't answer immediately, as if considering her question. Finally, it said, "This is not an ending, Elena. It is an opportunity."

The words sent a shiver down her spine. She tried to understand, but her thoughts felt slow, as if wading through water. "What kind of opportunity?" she asked hesitantly.

"To see beyond," the voice replied. "To understand what lies beneath the surface of your life, and to decide what comes next."

Suddenly, the whiteness began to change. It rippled like water disturbed by a breeze, and scenes began to emerge in its folds. Elena gasped as she saw the familiar streets of Korovets, the cobblestones glistening with morning dew. She saw herself as a young girl, running through the village square with her brother, Andriy, chasing her.

She felt a pang of emotion. Andriy had passed away years ago, a tragic accident that had left a hole in her family. Yet here he was, laughing, his cheeks flushed with the joy of childhood. She watched as her younger self tripped and fell, scraping her knee. Andriy was at her side in an instant, pulling her to her feet and brushing her off.

"You'll be okay," he said, his voice ringing clear in her memory. "You're tough, Lena."

The scene shifted, and Elena saw herself as a teenager, sitting on the steps of the schoolhouse. She was crying, her hands covering her face. It had been the day her father left, walking out on the family without a word of explanation. She remembered the crushing sense of abandonment, the way her mother had tried to hold things together but couldn't quite hide her own heartbreak.

Other moments came and went—her first job at the textile factory, the night her grandmother passed away, the quiet evenings spent alone in her apartment. Each memory carried a weight, a thread that wove together the tapestry of her life.

"You have lived with much pain," the voice said, breaking the silence. "Yet you have endured. Do you see the strength within you?"

Elena felt tears streaming down her cheeks. She hadn't thought of herself as strong—just someone who kept going because there was no other choice. But as she looked at these fragments of her life, she began to see what the voice meant.

"I never thought about it like that," she admitted.

The whiteness rippled again, and the scenes vanished. Now, Elena found herself standing in a forest. The air was cool and filled with the sound of rustling leaves. A path stretched out before her, winding through the trees.

"This is your journey," the voice said. "You may walk forward, or you may return."

"Return to what?" Elena asked, her voice barely a whisper.

"To your life," the voice replied. "There is still much for you to do, should you choose to go back."

Elena's heart ached at the thought of returning. The weight of her struggles, the monotony of her days—it was all so exhausting. Here, in this strange, peaceful realm, she felt free. But the voice's words lingered in her mind. Was there truly more for her to do?

As she stood at the edge of the path, a figure appeared in the distance. It was her mother, standing under the shade of a great oak tree. Her mother smiled, her face glowing with warmth and love. Elena's breath caught in her throat.

"Mom?" she called out, taking a step forward.

Her mother raised a hand, beckoning her closer. "Lena," she said softly, her voice carrying over the wind. "You have so much life left to live. Don't be afraid to go back."

Tears welled in Elena's eyes. "But what if I fail? What if I can't...?"

Her mother shook her head, her expression kind but firm. "You've never failed, my daughter. You've only ever tried, and that is enough. Go back, Lena. Live."

Elena hesitated, her heart torn. She looked down the path, then back at her mother. The forest seemed to hum with quiet anticipation, as if waiting for her decision.

Finally, she closed her eyes and took a deep breath. When she opened them again, she nodded. "I'll go back."

The forest began to dissolve, the light growing brighter and brighter until it consumed everything.

When Elena opened her eyes, she was lying on a hospital bed, a mask over her face delivering oxygen. The harsh fluorescent lights of the room stung her eyes, and the sounds of machines beeping filled her ears.

"She's awake!" a voice exclaimed. A nurse appeared by her side, her face breaking into a relieved smile. "You're okay, Miss. You made it."

Elena blinked, her mind struggling to catch up. Slowly, the events of the night came rushing back—the smoke, the fire, the escape. And the place she had been.

She looked out the window, where the first light of dawn was breaking over the village. For the first time in years, she felt a strange sense of purpose, a spark of hope. She didn't know what lay ahead, but she knew one thing: she was ready to face it.

24

The Weight of Shadows

Luise stared out the window of her tiny room, the bare walls of the orphanage pressing in on her like a suffocating blanket. The rain drummed against the glass, each drop sliding down as if it carried the weight of her memories. She pulled her knees to her chest, curling into herself as the shadows of her past danced in her mind.

At only 19 years old, Luise felt like a lifetime of pain had aged her beyond her years. Her childhood had been carved away piece by piece, each loss leaving a scar she couldn't hide.

The first fracture came when she was 11. Her father, the anchor of her small world, walked out the door and never came back. She had stood at the top of the stairs, clutching the wooden banister as her parents' voices echoed through the house below.

"It's not my fault you've let yourself go, Marta," her father had said coldly, his voice cutting through the air like a knife.

"And it's not my fault you've fallen for some cheap, younger fling!" her mother had screamed back, her voice breaking with fury and despair.

Luise didn't understand all the words at the time, but she felt their weight. When the door slammed shut and her father's car roared down the street, she knew he wasn't coming back.

Her mother, Marta, had crumbled under the weight of his departure. At first, it was subtle—an extra glass of wine at dinner, long sighs as she stared blankly at the television. But soon, the wine bottles multiplied, and the sighs turned into rants. Marta's grief became a constant storm, with Luise caught in its eye.

"He left us for *her*," Marta would slur, pointing at no one in particular. "Do you know what that feels like, Luise? To be tossed aside like garbage?"

Luise didn't know what to say. She was just a child, desperate for her mother's love, but all she got was bitterness and blame. Marta began eating more, using food to fill the void her husband had left. The woman who had once danced with Luise in the kitchen now barely moved from the couch, her sadness weighing her down both figuratively and literally.

Birthdays came and went with little fanfare. One year, when Luise turned 13, she mustered the courage to ask for a gift—a simple sketchbook. Her mother had laughed bitterly.

"Do you think we're made of money, Luise? Do you think I can just *pretend* everything is fine?"

Luise didn't ask again.

The final fracture came when Luise was 15. She had returned home from school to find the house eerily silent. Her mother, usually half-asleep on the couch, wasn't there. A chill ran down Luise's spine as she called out, her voice echoing in the empty house.

She found Marta in the bathroom, slumped on the floor, an empty bottle of cleaning fluid in her hand. The acrid smell burned Luise's nose, but what broke her was the look on her mother's face—regret etched into every line.

"I'm sorry, Luise," her mother had whispered, her voice weak. "I... I didn't mean for it to end like this."

Luise screamed for help, but by the time the ambulance arrived, it was too late. Her mother's regret came too late, leaving Luise alone in a world that had already taken so much from her.

The orphanage was cold, impersonal. The staff tried their best, but Luise felt like just another name on their endless list of lost children. The other kids avoided her; they could sense her sadness like a storm cloud that hung over her wherever she went.

At school, it wasn't much better. Luise kept her head down, afraid that if anyone got too close, they'd see the jagged pieces of her broken life. She became a ghost, drifting through the days, waiting for time to pass but never truly living.

Now, as the rain continued to fall outside, Luise felt the crushing weight of it all. She had tried to move on, to forget, but the memories were always there, clawing at her like shadows she couldn't escape.

She had no one to turn to, no family, no friends. The world felt vast and empty, and she was just a speck, insignificant and alone. She often wondered if her mother had been right to give up. Maybe life was just too hard, too cruel.

But somewhere, deep inside, a small voice whispered to her. It wasn't loud, but it was persistent.

You've survived this far. Don't let it win.

The voice was faint, like a flickering candle in the darkness. Luise didn't know if she could trust it, but it was there, refusing to be snuffed out.

That night, as the rain slowed to a drizzle, Luise made a decision. She didn't know if she had the strength to overcome her pain, but she was tired of letting it define her. She reached for the notebook she kept hidden under her bed—a cheap, spiral-bound journal she'd bought with the little money she had saved.

Opening it to a blank page, she began to write. At first, the words came slowly, hesitant, but soon they poured out, raw and unfiltered. She wrote about her father leaving, her mother's descent into despair, the loneliness that had consumed her life. She wrote until her hand ached and the pages were filled with her pain.

When she finished, she closed the notebook and held it to her chest. For the first time in years, she felt a tiny flicker of relief. The pain was still there, but writing it down had made it feel less overwhelming, as if she had taken a step toward reclaiming her life.

Luise didn't know what the future held, but she knew she didn't want to end up like her mother—drowning in sorrow, unable to see a way out. She wanted to find a reason to keep going, even if it was just a small one.

As the first rays of dawn broke through the clouds, Luise sat by the window and watched the world wake up. It wasn't much, but it was something. And for now, that was enough.

The days grew colder as Christmas approached, each passing hour a reminder of how alone Luise felt. The orphanage halls were decorated with cheerful paper snowflakes and strings of tinsel, but to her, it all felt hollow. Christmas wasn't a season of joy; it was a glaring spotlight on the family she didn't have, the love she didn't feel.

She tried to distract herself, throwing herself into her studies at university. But even there, the weight of her life seemed inescapable. She had failed two exams, her professors shaking their heads with the same disinterest she had come to expect.

Her boyfriend—if she could even call him that anymore—had left a few weeks earlier, claiming he "needed space." His departure mirrored her father's so closely it was almost laughable. "I'm not good for you, Luise," he had said, avoiding her eyes. The words stung, not because of their truth, but because of how little fight he had shown. Just like her father. Just like everyone.

The loneliness was unbearable, but she clung to a faint hope that writing to her father might bring some comfort. She had spent days drafting a letter, pouring her heart onto the page. She didn't ask for much—just a reply, a sign that she mattered to him. But days turned into weeks, and her letter went unanswered.

On Christmas Eve, Luise sat in her tiny room, staring at the ceiling as the muffled laughter of the other orphans drifted through the walls. They were celebrating in the dining hall, exchanging small gifts and singing carols. She couldn't bring herself to join them.

Her thoughts spiraled. She thought about her mother, slumped on the bathroom floor, her father walking out the door, her boyfriend's empty promises. Her mind replayed every failure, every rejection, until it felt like the walls of the room were closing in on her.

She reached for the bottle of pills on her nightstand, her hand trembling. Her heart ached in a way that felt unbearable, like a weight she could never lift. "What's the point?" she whispered to the silence around her.

One pill. Then another. And another. She didn't remember how many she took. She just remembered the overwhelming desire to escape the pain, to stop feeling so utterly lost.

When she closed her eyes, it wasn't darkness that greeted her but a strange, gentle light. She felt herself floating, weightless, as though she were shedding the heaviness of her body.

She opened her eyes to find herself standing in a place unlike anything she had ever seen. The air shimmered with a golden glow, and a sense of peace washed over her, unlike anything she had ever felt.

It wasn't silence that surrounded her, but a kind of stillness, as if the world itself had paused to listen.

"Am I dead?" she asked, her voice echoing in the vast, glowing expanse.

"No," a voice answered. It was neither male nor female, neither loud nor soft. It was simply there, resonating within her. "You are between."

"Between what?" she asked, her heart pounding despite the calm around her.

"Life and death. You have come close, but your time is not yet over."

The words wrapped around her like a warm embrace, yet they also sent a ripple of fear through her. "Why? Why bring me here? I have nothing left!"

The light shifted, softening, as though responding to her pain. "Because your story is not finished, Luise. There is more for you to do, more for you to be."

Tears filled her eyes, spilling over as she shook her head. "I've lost everything. My family, my friends, my future. There's nothing left for me."

The voice was silent for a moment, as if letting her words settle. Then it spoke again, gentle but firm. "You carry much pain, but you are not alone. Look closer, and you will see."

The light rippled, and scenes began to emerge, as if projected onto the golden expanse. She saw the orphanage director, a stern but kind woman who had given her extra tutoring sessions after her failed exams. She saw one of the younger girls at the orphanage, a shy 10-year-old who always smiled when Luise shared her sketchbook. She saw her professor, leaving a note on her desk encouraging her not to give up.

The voice spoke again. "You have touched lives, even in your pain. The smallest acts of kindness, the tiniest moments of connection—they matter more than you realize."

Luise sobbed, the weight of her emotions breaking free. "I don't know if I can keep going. I don't know how."

"You don't have to know," the voice replied. "You only have to take one step. And then another. You are stronger than you believe."

The light began to fade, and Luise felt herself being pulled back, the warmth and peace slipping away.

"No," she cried out, reaching for the light. "Please don't send me back. I'm not ready."

"You are ready," the voice said. "Because you are not alone. And you are loved, even when you cannot see it."

The words echoed in her mind as everything went dark.

Luise awoke to the harsh glare of fluorescent lights and the sound of voices around her. She was in a hospital bed, her body heavy and sluggish. A nurse stood by her side, her expression a mix of relief and concern.

"You're awake," the nurse said softly. "We were worried about you."

Luise blinked, her mind hazy. The memories of what had happened—the pills, the light, the voice—flooded back. She touched her chest, feeling the faint beat of her heart, and let out a shaky breath.

It hadn't been a dream. She knew that in her soul.

In the days that followed, Luise began to rebuild, piece by piece. She spoke to a counselor at the orphanage, sharing her story for the first time. She started journaling again, this time not just about her pain but about the glimmers of hope she had seen.

The holidays passed, and while they were still bittersweet, she found moments of light—a child's laughter, a kind word from a stranger, the realization that she wasn't as alone as she had thought.

Luise didn't have all the answers, and she still carried the scars of her past. But she also carried something new: a sense of purpose, however faint.

Her story wasn't over. And for the first time in a long time, she felt ready to see where it would go next.

25

A Taste of Trouble

Ethan Grey stood at the edge of the brightly lit room, scanning the crowd with a wary eye. The hum of chatter and bursts of laughter filled the air, punctuated by the occasional clink of glasses. It was his colleague Mia's birthday, and she had insisted on a party at the office after hours. The long conference table had been transformed into a feast of brightly frosted cupcakes, savory finger foods, and a center-piece—a large, ornate cake crowned with golden candles.

He shifted his weight, glancing at the clock. Social gatherings weren't his forte, especially ones centered on food. For Ethan, every bite was a calculated risk, every meal an exercise in vigilance. His peanut allergy wasn't just an inconvenience—it was a life-or-death matter.

"Come on, Ethan, live a little!" Mia teased, appearing beside him with a paper plate in hand. "It's just cake. No one's allergic to cake."

Ethan offered a polite smile. "It's not the cake, Mia. It's what's in it."

"Relax," she said, nudging him. "I made sure there's nothing weird in it. You deserve a treat."

The cake did look appealing. Layers of sponge and cream, delicately piped frosting—Mia's insistence made him second-guess his caution.

Besides, he trusted her. She knew about his allergy. Surely, if there was any risk, she'd have warned him.

"Alright," he said, his voice betraying his hesitation. He picked up a small slice and took a tentative bite.

The first taste was sweet and creamy, the texture melting on his tongue. A faint nuttiness lingered, but he dismissed it as part of the complex flavors. For a moment, he allowed himself to enjoy it, sinking into the rare pleasure of indulgence.

The room buzzed around Ethan, but he hardly noticed. The cake was surprisingly good, and he allowed himself to relax, savoring the treat. It was rare for him to indulge like this, constantly vigilant about hidden dangers in his food. For once, he felt normal—just another person enjoying a celebration. Minutes later, he felt it.

At first, it was subtle: an itch at the back of his throat. He cleared his throat softly, brushing it off as a tickle. But then, the itch deepened, spreading like an unseen hand tightening its grip. A flush of heat crept up his neck, and his chest began to feel heavy, as though an invisible weight was pressing down.

His pulse quickened as realization set in. His body was reacting. Panic threatened to cloud his thoughts, but he forced himself to stay calm. Breathing carefully, he glanced around the room, searching for his bag. His epinephrine injector was always with him—always—except...

He felt his stomach sink. The bag wasn't by his chair where he usually kept it. He had left it in the car, thinking he wouldn't need it for a simple office party. How could he have been so careless?

Mia approached him, laughing. "Hey, what did I tell you? It's good, right?" Her smile faltered as she noticed his pale face and the beads of sweat forming on his brow. "Ethan? Are you okay?"

His voice came out hoarse. "Mia... what's in the cake?"

She blinked, confused. "Just the usual. Flour, eggs, sugar, butter... oh, and a little peanut butter for flavor. Why?"

The room seemed to tilt. Peanut butter. His vision blurred as adrenaline and fear surged through him.

"I'm... allergic," he managed to choke out before a fit of coughing overtook him.

Mia's face turned white. "Oh my God! Ethan, I—I didn't know. I thought you meant tree nuts, like almonds or something."

Ethan stumbled back, gripping the edge of the table for support. The crowd noticed the commotion, and murmurs of concern rippled through the room.

A man in the crowd shouted, "He's having an allergic reaction! Someone call 911!"

Ethan's breathing grew shallow, each inhale a struggle against the tightness in his chest. His hands trembled as he clutched at his throat, trying to force air into his lungs. A tingling numbness began to creep up his face and arms.

"Where's your EpiPen?" Mia asked frantically, shaking him slightly.

"Car," Ethan rasped, his voice barely audible.

"Stay with us!" another voice said as someone guided him to sit down. The world around him became a chaotic blur of voices and motion. Someone fumbled with their phone, shouting into it for an ambulance. Others hovered helplessly, unsure of what to do.

"I'll get it!" a young intern yelled, bolting out of the room toward the parking lot.

Seconds stretched into what felt like hours. Ethan's vision narrowed, black spots dancing at the edges. His thoughts turned hazy, drifting between panic and resignation. **This is it.** He could feel his body shutting down.

Suddenly, the door burst open. The intern, breathless and wide-eyed, held up Ethan's injector. "I've got it!"

"Give it here!" shouted a middle-aged woman who stepped forward. "I know how to use it."

Ethan felt the sharp jab in his thigh, followed by the rush of medication flooding his system. The effect wasn't instant, but within moments, his airway began to open, and he sucked in a ragged breath. Relief washed over him like a wave, but his body remained shaky and weak.

The ambulance arrived minutes later, the paramedics quickly taking over. They assessed Ethan, stabilized him, and loaded him onto a stretcher for transport to the hospital. As he was wheeled out, he managed a weak smile at Mia, who was still pale and trembling with guilt.

At the hospital, doctors confirmed that he had experienced anaphylactic shock—a potentially fatal reaction. They commended the quick action of his colleagues, explaining that without the injection, the outcome could have been dire.

Later, lying in the hospital bed, Ethan replayed the events in his mind. A single lapse in judgment had brought him to the brink of disaster. He vowed never to let his guard down again.

When Mia visited, her eyes red from crying, Ethan offered her a faint smile. "It's okay," he said. "I should have checked. It's my responsibility too."

Mia shook her head. "No, I should have asked. I didn't know how serious it was. I'm so sorry."

Ethan reached out, gripping her hand. "Let's just make sure this doesn't happen to anyone else."

In the weeks that followed, Ethan became a vocal advocate for allergy awareness. He shared his story at work and in his community, emphasizing the importance of labeling ingredients and understanding the severity of food allergies.

The experience left him shaken but also more determined than ever to protect himself and others. He learned that vigilance was essential, but so was forgiveness—both for himself and for those who made honest mistakes.

Because sometimes, it's not just about surviving the moment. It's about what you do with the second chance.

26

Between Shadows and Light

Sergeant Liam Carter sat on the porch of his modest home, the morning sun casting long shadows across the neatly trimmed lawn. A steaming cup of coffee rested on the weathered table beside him, untouched. His eyes were fixed on the horizon, but his mind was far away, back in a place of endless dust and sun-blanched rocks. Afghanistan.

The sound of children laughing in the distance pulled him briefly back to the present. He took a deep breath, but it felt shallow, as if the weight of memory pressed on his chest. Today, the memories were sharper, more vivid. His hand drifted to his thigh, tracing the jagged scar beneath his jeans—a constant reminder of the day his world changed forever. It had been a routine patrol, or at least that's what they'd called it.

Liam was 28 years old, lean and sharp-eyed, leading a small unit through the rugged terrain of a remote Afghan village. The sun beat down mercilessly, and the weight of his gear felt heavier with every step. His team had been tasked with gathering intel on an insurgent network rumored to operate in the area.

The village was eerily quiet. Too quiet. The kind of quiet that set every nerve on edge. Liam scanned the rooftops and windows for movement, his rifle at the ready.

"Stay sharp," he murmured into his radio. "Something's off."

Corporal Jackson, his second-in-command, was a few steps behind him, muttering about how much he hated the quiet. Private Torres, the youngest in the unit, was nervously scanning the ground. "IEDs," the kid had said more times than Liam could count that day. "They bury them in the dumbest places."

As they moved through the village, Liam's instincts prickled. He stopped abruptly, raising a fist to signal the team to halt. The air felt charged, like the moment before a lightning strike.

And then it happened.

His boot pressed down on something hard. A click, almost inaudible, vibrated through his sole. The world seemed to freeze. For a heartbeat, he didn't move, his brain racing to confirm what his senses were screaming.

"IED," he whispered hoarsely, his voice barely carrying over the oppressive silence.

The team froze, their faces masks of fear and determination. Jackson's eyes locked onto Liam's foot, widening in horror. "Sarge"

The explosion cut him off.

The world erupted in sound and fury, a deafening roar that obliterated everything else. Liam felt himself hurled into the air, his body weightless, spinning like a ragdoll. The sensation was surreal a slow-motion detachment from reality. Dust and debris filled the air, blotting out the sun.

When Liam opened his eyes, he wasn't in Afghanistan. He wasn't sure where he was. A soft golden light bathed the landscape, its source untraceable. The ground beneath him felt like solid air, impossibly smooth and warm. The horizon stretched endlessly, blurring into the distance. He wasn't alone.

Figures emerged from the light, their faces familiar and haunting. Sergeant Phillips, his old mentor who had died in an ambush years ago, stepped forward with a grim smile. Beside him was Corporal Mason, who had taken a sniper's bullet on Liam's first deployment.

"Phillips?" Liam's voice was steady, but his heart raced. "Mason?"

"You made it further than we did," Phillips said, his voice carrying an edge of approval.

Liam's chest tightened. "Why am I here?"

"You stepped too close," Mason replied, his tone light, as though they were back in the barracks.

"This isn't real," Liam said, shaking his head. "This is... a dream, or—"

"Does it feel like a dream?" Phillips interrupted, his gaze piercing. "You're at a crossroads, Carter. You've got a choice to make."

Liam felt a tug behind him and turned. The golden light gave way to a deep shadow, a void that seemed to pulse with life. It was silent, yet it called to him, tugging at something deep within.

"You're not done," a voice said, softer this time. Liam turned again and saw another figure. His mother, her hair tied back the way she always wore it when he was a boy. Her smile was gentle, but her eyes brimmed with tears.

"Mom?" His voice cracked. "What... what's happening?"

She stepped closer, her hand brushing his cheek. "You've done so much, Liam. But your story isn't over. You have to go back."

Liam felt torn, the light and shadow pulling him in opposite directions. The peace of this place was intoxicating, a balm for his weary soul. Yet, something deep within him stirred—a need to fight, to return, to finish what he had started.

"I don't want to leave," he admitted. "But I can't stay."

Phillips nodded. "Then fight, Carter. Fight like hell."

The light grew brighter, overwhelming everything. Liam felt himself falling, the golden warmth fading into cold and darkness.

When he opened his eyes again, he was back in the dust and chaos of Afghanistan. The ringing in his ears was deafening, and pain radiated through his entire body. He tried to move but couldn't. His teammates were shouting, their voices muffled.

"Stay with us, Sarge!" Jackson's voice broke through the haze.

Liam wanted to speak, to tell them he was okay, but the words wouldn't come. He slipped into darkness again, waking hours later in a hospital bed, the faint hum of machinery filling the air.

The road to recovery was long and grueling. Liam spent months in physical therapy, learning to walk again on a prosthetic leg. The scars on his body were nothing compared to the ones in his mind. But the memory of that near-death experience stayed with him, a strange comfort in his darkest moments.

He had been given a second chance, and he was determined to make it count. Liam began speaking to other veterans, sharing his story of survival and resilience. He started a support group, helping those who had seen the same shadows and light find their way back to life.

Liam stood once more on his porch, watching the sunset paint the sky in hues of gold and crimson. The scars, the memories—they would always be a part of him. But he had made peace with them.

Life, he realized, was not about the shadows that tried to consume him but about the light that guided him through. And he wasn't done walking. Not yet.

27

Meeting The Universe

Jason Hartley was a man whose words shaped worlds. A prolific author with over a dozen novels to his name, he had spent most of his life conjuring realms and lives that captivated millions. Yet, for all his literary achievements, Jason had a failing that his readers could never see: a self-destructive lifestyle fueled by excessive drinking, smoking, and a stubborn refusal to heed his deteriorating health.

At 42, Jason's body began to betray him. Years of unhealthy habits had culminated in chronic chest pains and shortness of breath—symptoms he ignored until the night his body finally forced him to pay attention. He had been at his desk, struggling with the first draft of his next novel, when a searing pain gripped his chest and radiated down his arm. His vision blurred, and the world seemed to collapse into a tunnel of shadows before everything went dark.

Jason's next conscious thought was not one of pain but of profound peace. He found himself in a place he could only describe as ethereal. It wasn't a physical space but an expanse of light and warmth, filled with a presence that felt both alien and deeply familiar. He saw no pearly gates or angelic beings, but he felt an overwhelming sense of connection—to himself, to others, to the very fabric of existence. And then came the voices.

They weren't voices in the traditional sense but impressions, waves of understanding that seemed to emanate from every direction. Jason felt his life unfurl before him—not as a series of events but as a tapestry of moments that rippled outward, touching lives he hadn't even realized he'd influenced. He felt the weight of his regrets, the opportunities he'd squandered, but also the joy he'd brought to others through his stories.

Just as Jason began to feel at home in this otherworldly place, a force pulled him back. It was as if he were being reeled in by an unseen hand, the light fading, the warmth receding, until he woke with a jolt. Harsh fluorescent lights greeted his eyes, and the beeping of monitors filled his ears. He was in a hospital, surrounded by concerned faces. A nurse informed him that he had suffered a massive heart attack and had been clinically dead for nearly three minutes before being resuscitated.

Those three minutes haunted Jason in the days and weeks that followed. He couldn't shake the memory of that luminous expanse and the insights he'd gained. The experience left him questioning everything he thought he knew about life, death, and his place in the universe. More than that, it left him with an unshakable conviction: he had been given a second chance, and he couldn't squander it.

Jason's first step toward reclaiming his life was to quit his biggest weakness - the cigarettes and whiskey that had once been his constant companions were now symbols of his old, self-destructive self. He embraced a healthier lifestyle, started therapy, and reconnected with friends and family he had neglected for years. But the most profound change came in his writing.

For months after his near-death experience, Jason struggled to put pen to paper. The novel he had been working on before his heart attack felt trivial in light of what he had experienced. He abandoned it, deciding instead to write a memoir—a deeply personal account of his journey to the brink of death and back. He called it *Meeting The Universe*.

Writing the memoir was cathartic but also excruciating. Jason had to confront parts of himself he had spent years avoiding: his fear of vulnerability, his guilt over failed relationships, and his shame at having taken his life and talents for granted. But as he poured his soul onto the page, he found a clarity and purpose he had never known before.

Meeting The Universe was unlike anything Jason had ever written. It was raw, honest, and deeply reflective, weaving his near-death experience with meditations on life, love, and the human condition. He wrote about the light, the voices, and the tapestry of connections he had seen, but he also wrote about the lessons he had learned since his return: the importance of living authentically, of nurturing relationships, and of leaving the world better than he found it.

When Jason finished the manuscript, he felt a sense of fulfillment he hadn't experienced in years. He sent it to his agent, who was initially skeptical of the departure from Jason's usual genre. But after reading it, she was moved to tears and insisted it was the best thing he had ever written. The book was published six months later and became an instant bestseller.

Readers from all walks of life connected with Jason's story. Letters poured in from people who had faced their own brushes with death, who had lost loved ones, or who were simply searching for meaning in their lives. Jason's words had touched them in a way that his novels never had, and he found himself at the center of a global conversation about life, death, and what lies beyond.

But for Jason, the true measure of success wasn't the book sales or the accolades. It was the way his life had changed. He had mended his relationship with his estranged sister, Sarah, who had been one of his fiercest critics. He had found love with a fellow author, Emily, who admired his courage and vulnerability. And he had discovered a sense of peace and gratitude that had eluded him for most of his life.

In the years that followed, Jason continued to write, but he never returned to fiction. Instead, he devoted himself to exploring the themes that had emerged in *Meeting The Universe*. He wrote about resilience, forgiveness, and the power of human connection. He became a sought-after speaker, sharing his story with audiences around the world and inspiring others to live their lives with greater intention.

Jason often reflected on the luminous expanse he had seen during his near-death experience. He didn't know if it was heaven, an alternate dimension, or a construct of his brain in its final moments. But he knew it had changed him in ways he could never fully articulate. It had given him a second chance not just at life but at truly living.

As he sat at his desk one sunny morning, pen in hand, Jason felt a familiar warmth wash over him. It wasn't the otherworldly light he had seen during those three minutes, but something equally profound: the light of a life well-lived, illuminated by love, purpose, and the enduring power of the human spirit.

www.ingramcontent.com/pod-product-compliance
Lightning Source LLC
LaVergne TN
LVHW011005200726
843509LV00011B/996